Heali
wounded tiger

Also by the same author

Managing the Malaysian Economy:
Challenges & Prospects
Strengthening the Malaysian Economy:
Policy Changes & Reforms

RAMON V. NAVARATNAM

Healing the wounded tiger

How the
TURMOIL
is Reshaping
MALAYSIA

Pelanduk
Publications
www.pelanduk.com

Published by
Pelanduk Publications (M) Sdn Bhd
(Co. No. 113307-W)
12 Jalan SS13/3E
Subang Jaya Industrial Estate
47500 Subang Jaya
Selangor Darul Ehsan, Malaysia

Address all correspondence to
Pelanduk Publications (M) Sdn Bhd
P.O. Box 8265, 46785 Kelana Jaya
Selangor Darul Ehsan, Malaysia

Check out our website at *www.pelanduk.com*
e-mail: *mypp@tm.net.my*

Perpustakaan Negara Malaysia   Cataloguing-in-Publication Data

Navaratnam, Ramon V.
    Healing the wounded tiger: how the turmoil is reshaping
    Malaysia / Ramon V. Navaratnam
    Includes index
    ISBN 967-978-674-9
    1. Malaysia—Economic conditions. 2. Malaysia—Economic
    policy. 3. Financial crisis—Malaysia. 4. Currency question—
    Malaysia. I. Title.
    338.9595

Printed in Malaysia by
Percetakan Soonly Trading

*"For my loving family,
and for all Malaysians and others who care to
read and understand the heady and exciting changes
taking place in the Malaysian economy today."*
Ramon V. Navaratnam

CONTENTS

FOREWORD

Dato' Mustapa Mohamed
Second Finance Minister, Malaysia

I am delighted to recommend Tan Sri Ramon V. Navaratnam's third book on the Malaysian economy. His first and second books, *Managing the Malaysian Economy: Challenges & Prospects* and *Strengthening the Malaysian Economy: Policy Changes & Reforms*, have been well received.

Healing the Wounded Tiger: How the Turmoil is Reshaping Malaysia comes at a time when the Malaysian economy is going through a difficult phase consequent to the currency attacks and the economic turmoil that beset us after eight years of unprecedented high economic growth and price stability.

The economic commentaries in this book though critical of the socio-economic developments and issues over the last few months are constructive.

I may not agree with all of the author's views but I appreciate them as valued feedback from an honest Malaysian nationalist. These commentaries are particularly useful as they reflect the subtle insights of an economist who served with dedication in the Malaysian Treasury for most of his 30-year career in the Malaysian Civil Service. He also brings to this analysis of public policy the knowledge he has gained both from the government and the private sector. He was the CEO of Bank Buruh (now known as BSN Commercial Bank) and is now Corporate Adviser to the SungeiWay group of companies.

I wish there were more economists like him, who would write frankly on the Malaysian economy as reflected in this book.

I am glad that all royalties from the sale of this book, as his previous books, will go towards charity. The royalties from his first book were given to a poor boy who underwent hole-in-the-heart surgery. I believe this book will achieve its objective which, as Navaratnam asserts, is to encourage debate on the Malaysian economy.

I would like to congratulate Navaratnam on his effort and hope that his book will stimulate constructive discussion on the Malaysian economy.

Dato' Mustapa Mohamed
Second Finance Minister, Malaysia

PREFACE

AS we approach the new millennium in these tumultuous times, and as nations in the Asian region and elsewhere learn to cope with the fallout of the financial crisis and grapple to find solutions to economic ills, I have written this book for two reasons.

First, the overwhelming success and positive response to my first two books, *Managing the Malaysian Economy: Challenges & Prospects* and *Strengthening the Malaysian Economy: Policy Changes & Reforms*, inspired and spurred me to work on a book on reviving an economy in crisis.

Second, to stimulate public discussion and debate on the economic and financial situation in Malaysia and its prospects for recovery. By encouraging transparency, accountability, open debate and frank criticism, we will become more confident in our pursuit of a more determined spirit to face the challenges of greater globalisation and liberalisation as we approach a new century and a new millennium.

I always believed that a well-informed public will assist the government in devising policies and strategies that are more relevant and pragmatic. More public discussion of economic and financial matters will also garner more support for our national efforts to overcome the serious socio-economic problems resulting from the current financial crisis, caused mainly by currency speculation and manipulation.

By focusing on our strengths and weaknesses, as well as the external challenges confronting us now and in the years ahead, this book suggests possible solutions to problems plaguing the economy, and hopes to encourage intelligent discussion of and debate on how to revive, manage and strengthen the Malaysian economy so as to sustain economic growth towards achieving industrialised-nation status by 2020.

It is in this spirit that I have written his book, and I hope it will make an important contribution, however small, to a better understanding of the grave international and domestic socio-economic crisis confronting us all, and what we can and should do about it.

However, this book would not have materialised if not for the encouragement and insights of a few individuals: Ng Tieh Chuan and Eric C. Forbes of Pelanduk Publications, for encouraging me to undertake the task of rewriting and expanding my commentaries on current economic and financial developments in Malaysia, and I am grateful for their constructive comments and suggestions, and to my secretary Haema for her patience.

And last but not least, as always, my gratitude to my dearest wife Samala, not only for her understanding and steadfast support, but also for her quiet inspiration.

Ramon V. Navaratnam

INTRODUCTION

DESPITE the relatively sound management that earned many of the East Asian tiger economies the envy of industrialised economies, they are now severely wounded. Over-confidence somehow led to a great degree of complacency that brought about some incompetence in economic and financial management, while a slackening vigilance exposed them to the ruthless exploitation of their vulnerability by currency speculators and manipulators, who are unfortunately not yet subject to the normal regulations applicable to world trade and investment. But the wounded Malaysian tiger is in the process of healing and is on the road to recovery.

It has been more than a year since the *de facto* devaluation of the Thai baht which led to the Great Asian Economic and Financial Crisis and the temporary stalemate of the much-vaunted Asian Miracle. While governments are trying their best to salvage their troubled economies and stabilise their currencies, the average citizen is trying to understand and cope with the economic fallout. Some of the fallout from the crisis include retrenchments, salary cuts, and diminishing purchasing power as a result of widespread inflation, higher costs of doing business, bankruptcies, etc. The speed at which the tiger economies and their currencies deteriorated caught most of us off-guard.

Caught in the eye of the storm, the Malaysian economy, which had enjoyed spectacular growth for eight consecutive years, was jolted from its euphoria in July 1997, when the vicious contagion effect arising from the devaluation of the Thai baht sent East Asian currencies and stockmarkets plummeting to a nadir never before experienced.

It is essential that we take stock of the crisis and ask why and how this breathtaking march to prosperity was brought to a grinding halt by the financial crisis. *What were the probable causes of the crisis and what lessons can we draw from it?* We need to thoroughly review what really happened, or else we will never learn from it.

Malaysia's efforts at rehabilitating its economy to regain investor confidence should diffuse concerns as to whether the imposition of selective capital and currency controls on September 1, 1998 would adversely affect the flow of FDI into Malaysia. Malaysian Prime Minister Dato' Seri Dr Mahathir Mohamad has assured foreign investors that these controls do not pose any hindrance to FDI inflows as there would continue to be no restrictions in the repatriation of profits, dividends, capital and other proceeds.

Will Malaysia's policy of "insulating" itself "behind a firewall of capital and currency controls and a fixed exchange rate" defy the odds and jumpstart its economy?

The capital and currency controls introduced on September 1, 1998 have successfully protected Malaysia from further attacks by unscrupulous currency speculators and manipulators. Yes, capital controls will be disastrous, but only to the speculators who have vested interests in keeping the currency markets wide open for them to attack mercilessly.

It is wrong of critics to assume that the capital and currency controls would be a permanent fixture on the Malaysian economic landscape. When international monetary reforms are introduced and unscrupulous currency manipulators are brought under some degree of supervision, only then would it be safe for Malaysia to fully reopen its capital and currency markets once again.

Some analysts have claimed that the effects of the controls imposed by Malaysia would be detrimental to the Malaysian economy and that the measures taken would hurt other countries which are trying to keep their financial markets open, because controls, they say, would encourage capital flight. However, measures aimed at "insulating" the Malaysian economy from external volatility and speculation is worth the risk because it will allow the reduction of interest rates and help companies reduce their debt burdens and improve their earnings potential.

The assurance made by the United Nations Conference on Trade and Development (UNCTAD) that small developing countries have to resort to capital and currency controls to prevent socioeconomic disaster and political instability is a lesson in economics to those who would like to exploit the free-market paradigm for their own narrow self-interests.

There is no question of being misguided and misleading in our action. It is really a defence against external instability and resistance to currency attacks. If US President Bill Clinton and the Group of Seven (G7) countries—Britain, Canada, France, Germany, Italy, Japan and the United States, which dominate the International Monetary Fund (IMF), do not allow international monetary reforms to take place as a matter of urgency, these rich and powerful industrial countries will run the risk of recession and socio-political instability that will be brought about by the currency contagion, now moving to Latin America and even the United States.

Instead of being cynical of our measures, why doesn't George Soros push for constructive measures to tackle the problems brought about by the free-market regime? We believe in the prosper-thy-neighbour principle and a win-win situation for all in the free-trade equation, but currency manipulators are doing their best to undermine this philosophy. That is why we have to counter them or we will lose out at the end of the day. *Or perhaps this is the grand design of some countries?*

IMF First Deputy Managing Director Stanley Fischer is especially concerned with Malaysia's high-stake "experiment" with currency controls. During a news conference in Washington, DC, where Fischer unveiled the IMF's 1998 annual report on September 13, he told the audience that Malaysia's bold "experiment" with currency controls will cut the country off from the international monetary system and will not do much for its economy in the long term.

Fischer is concerned that the imposition of such measures may appear to succeed in the short term, but in the long term, it could drive away foreign investors and reduce opportunities for Malaysian companies to participate in the global market. "Malaysia's extraordinary growth had benefited from the international capital market, but the new measures that include fixing the Malaysian ringgit at RM3.80 to the US dollar would reduce the willingness of foreign companies to invest in the country." *But Fischer forgets that we do not intend to impose exchange controls permanently!*

Malaysia's currency controls could signal the start of a global backlash against the brand of bitter medicine to cure economic ills offered by the IMF. The likelihood of an immediate rush to emulate Malaysia's controls on foreign exchange seemed remote given the IMF's heavy involvement in Asia. But the depth and breadth of the emerging markets' crisis could portend a shift in attitudes on the merits of capital controls in emerging-market economies. This has happened in two great economies, China and Russia now! Other countries could follow suit.

By introducing capital and currency controls to shield its battered ringgit and its economy from currency manipulators and global financial instability, Malaysia took a giant step away from orthodoxy. As we progress, investors will see the rest of the world increasingly blending government, societal and market forces together. The complete domination of market forces in this process is now at its zenith. The type of government intervention now evident in Hong Kong (where the government bought shares aggressively in August 1998 to foil market manipulators) would soon no longer be criticised but seen as pragmatic and in the nation's interest. Global capital will thus realign itself accordingly. The philosophy and even "religion" of the unfettered free market will evolve into something more realistic and humane.

Malaysia should not be viewed as a model for Asian nations disaffected by more than a year of ineffective IMF policy intervention. However, the IMF's insistence on high real interest rates and full debt repayment to foreign creditor banks is condemning Asia to a lengthy recession similar to the Latin American debt crisis of the 1980s.

Despite instituting currency controls to curb speculative attacks on the ringgit, Malaysia has not "isolated" itself from the global economy. The perception that Malaysia has cut itself off from the mainstream of global economy, as widely reported in the Western press, must be corrected. Malaysia's ability to continue attracting long-term foreign capital would depend on whether it manages to dispel this inaccurate misperception of "isolation". We must convince the world that we are neither anti-business nor anti-market, and that we will continue to promote trade and foreign direct investment because we believe these conduits are essential for universal prosperity.

Though capital and currency controls and an easier monetary stance taken by the Malaysian government has put Malaysia on the road to economic recovery, there is, however, much more that can and need to be done to hasten recovery.

While lower interest rates and the several new measures will increase liquidity in the banking system and allow some breathing space for the economy to get back on its feet, more initiatives and reforms in the banking system are still needed. We need to hasten the process of restructuring our own banking and financial system to face the rising tide of globalisation and liberalisation. The pressure on us will rise at APEC summits and various other fora.

There is more scope for liberalisation in the banking and financial sector to allow for both the infusion of capital and expertise into the Malaysian financial system. Undeniably, this will contribute to the long-term stability of the overall economy. While we cannot allow for absolute liberalisation in the banking and financial system, greater relaxation of our current rules and regulations would certainly be welcomed, but at our own pace.

Furthermore, the scarce amount of funds that is being raised through special purpose vehicles such as Danaharta and Danamodal should be used to help high-priority enterprises that are able to contribute to the well-being of the economy. Such funds should not be used to rescue companies that are mismanaged.

Besides fixing a banking and financial system paralysed by bad debts and getting ailing institutions back on their feet, we must also look into the small- and medium-scale industries (SMIs), which are important to the economy. The stringent requirement of having 30 per cent *Bumiputera* representation before SMIs expand beyond the capital base of RM2.5 million has been fortunately relaxed until December 2000. But this new policy must be actively promoted in order to be fruitful.

Seeking IMF aid, to Dr Mahathir, was tantamount to surrendering the nation's economic sovereignty and he wasn't going to accept that. None of the earlier domestic packages of initiatives managed to stem the steep fall of the ringgit and the daily declines on the Kuala Lumpur Stock Exchange (KLSE). So Dr Mahathir introduced new measures independent of the IMF, through the National Economic Recovery Plan (NERP) and the 1999 Budget introduced on October 23, 1998. These measures are healing the wounded Malaysian tiger, which is now in the midst of recovery.

We believe that, given our political stability and strong will to combat recession, the Malaysian economy could very well lead the pack in Southeast Asia to recover in the near future.

Though the road ahead is fraught with pitfalls and challenges, we must strengthen our socio-economic resolve and resilience not only by overcoming our weaknesses and inefficiencies, but also by attempting to win global support to take irresponsible currency speculators and manipulators to task in a new international financial architecture.

The only way out of the economic and financial turmoil is to practice self-criticism and exercise a stronger political will to put as many policy measures as possible into action so that recovery will be attained at a quicker pace. Unfortunately, any hope of recovery will rests on three crucial assumptions: that the United States and Europe would remain economically buoyant, that the credit crunch in Japan will improve and that Russia and Brazil would not plunge the world into financial turbulence.

Chapter 1

LIMITED CHOICE
OF STRATEGIES FOR
ECONOMIC RECOVERY

IT has been more than a year since the onset of the currency crisis in mid-1997 in Thailand, and the economic meltdown has adversely affected the whole of Asia. Needless to say, Malaysia was not spared and was badly hit by the resultant fallout. This is probably the most trying time of our post-Independence period. Everyone wants to know when the Malaysian economy will really recover. *What stage of crisis are we in now? Have we seen the worst or are we still in the midst of the crisis?* There are, unfortunately, no easy answers to these questions.

I had earlier predicted that we would be emerging from the economic slowdown by the end of 1998. This expectation was based on the understanding that we would take tougher action to counter the economic slide. But, obviously, we have not been doing enough, especially from the foreign investors' point of view. *We are still experiencing a sense of denial, and as long as this "denial syndrome" persists, we will not recover fast enough.*

That is why the Malaysian ringgit and the stockmarket continue to be in a state of inertia, weak and sluggish, and we are now even experiencing negative growth rates. Confidence in the Malaysian economy is still at a low ebb. *Why is this so? And what does it take to restore confidence and facilitate economic recovery?*

Domestic Scenario

Since the fiscal and monetary measures introduced in March 1998, there has been no new major package of reforms. On the contrary, there continue to be more misgivings. Several companies have already gone under and many more are expected to follow suit. There are growing concerns that the authorities may want to rescue some companies and individuals, even at the expense of jeopardising minority interests.

There is also growing concern about the health of the Malaysian banking and financial system. Non-performing loans (NPLs) could go up substantially, if more companies collapse and thus fail to settle their debts. Then even some strong banks will be weakened. NPLs are now at about 10 per cent. But there are fears that they could rise to 15 per cent or more. (Once the NPLs of a bank reach a certain percentage determined by the central bank, no new loans are allowed to be issued anymore.) Most analysts, therefore, are waiting a little longer to paint a clearer picture of the state of health of our corporate sector. This will throw more light on the viability of our financial system. By then, all companies would have published their balance sheets as required by the Registrar of Companies (ROC), and then we will be able to observe the real state of corporate casualties.

Possible bailouts and bank weaknesses are two serious concerns of foreign financial analysts. Since they are the ones who determine the amount of foreign capital flowing into Malaysia, they could influence the rate of our recovery.

Foreign analysts believe that Taiwan, Hong Kong and Singapore will lead in the Asian economic recovery. Malaysia is expected to recover later, but they believe Thailand could move up and beat us if we are too slow in our reforms. But external developments could also have adverse effects on our prospects for early recovery. *For instance, what is going to happen to the other Asian economies?*

External Scenario

Our prospects for recovery will worsen if China devalues its currency or if Japan, the world's second-biggest economy after the United States, and by far Asia's largest, does not provide the necessary engine for growth in Asia. Japan's troubled economy—a bankrupt financial system, depressed consumer spending and falling prices—has fuelled fears that its recession could turn into a long-term depression, dragging others down with it. The United States is more concerned with the continuation of its own economic growth. It blames the Japanese for not doing as much as it should to revitalise its economy.

But the United States itself has done less than Japan to financially assist Asia. The United States has also not done much to hasten the pace of reform in the international financial architecture. Indeed, there is even a real problem in the US Congress to approve an allocation of US$18 billion needed to meet US obligations to the cash-starved IMF. This lack of US leadership at a time of international crisis is especially worrying. The Europeans too are preoccupied with the establishment of the new Euro currency. They have not done enough to improve the international financial architecture either.

For the West, alas, international financial reform is not their priority as they continue to gain from the *status quo*. After all, the major currency speculators come from the West and they pay huge taxes there. Never mind if it hurts the East.

The change in leadership in Indonesia, however, could bring greater financial stability and better prospects to Asia in the medium term. This is the most encouraging regional development. But then again, the continuing uncertainty in Indonesia remains a major concern in the immediate term.

What then can we do?

We have to do more for ourselves, rather than depend on others, to reverse our decline and accelerate our economic recovery as early as possible. Prime Minister Dato' Seri Dr Mahathir Mohamad made one of his most important speeches recently when he said: "Our weaknesses are due to our culture, which does not really stress hard work, seeking knowledge, moderation in life, adopting good values and other things." It is therefore crucial that we find ways of coping with the internal and external challenges confronting us. Since Malaysia is an open economy, we have to take into account foreigners' perceptions of us and make necessary adjustments as much as possible. If we don't, we will have to face the consequences of a slow inflow of both equity capital and foreign direct investment.

We cannot recover fast enough and sustain strong economic growth without adequate foreign investments. Our balance of payments position is weak, our reserves are low and now our Budget is under severe strain. So we have to do more to overcome the concerns of foreign investors in order to attract more long-term investment.

Unfortunately, we have limited choices at our disposal. That is why the establishment of an asset management company will provide a breakthrough to faster economic recovery. But it must operate professionally and without political persuasion. Then foreign investors will come back and our credit crunch will ease and interest rates could come down.

But we have to be careful not to borrow too much or we will have to pay the price later!

Foreign Expectations

What are the expectations of foreign investors of us? Basically, they want our markets to be made available to them on the basis of "national treatment". They want to have the same rights and privileges to do business in Malaysia as Malaysians have in our own country!

Indeed, the current discussions at the Organisation for Economic Cooperation and Development (OECD)—made up of the most developed and rich countries—aim to establish the Multilateral Agreement on Investment (MAI). This draft agreement seeks National Status for all rich and poor countries.

According to the MAI, all government licences, permits, land alienation, investment and government contracts must be made equally available to foreigners (just as they are made available to locals). This aim will be pursued at the World Trade Organisation (WTO). Understandably, there has been resistance from developing countries against the take-over and economic domination by the rich countries.

Nevertheless, the International Monetary Fund (IMF) has managed to insist on these concessions as their conditions for providing financial aid to South Korea, Indonesia and Thailand. Thus, the WTO has succeeded in using the IMF as a tool to achieve its aims. And those who dominate the WTO and the IMF are the rich and powerful industrial countries of the West!

Malaysia is one of the most lucrative markets for the West in the developing world. Hence, they want us to open our markets wide for them, regardless of the price we have to pay. The fact that we have resisted IMF interference so far is obnoxious to them. They want to know why they should not be able to *"gobble-ise"* some of our banks and financial institutions and then control our economy under the clarion call for "globalisation". For better or worse, the world's markets have become interlinked and interdependent.

I believe that many powerful vested interests in rich industrial countries will continue to discredit us through the mass media and the giant investment funds that they own, as long as they are not allowed to take over our banks and other critical financial institutions and businesses.

What then should our immediate and future strategies be?

First, we should continue to resist the IMF and its bungling, as it has done so in Indonesia and South Korea. The IMF chief Michel Camdessus says that we should not blame the doctor but the patient for neglecting to take the proper medicine. However, he must concede that the IMF doctors could have given the wrong medicine in the first place and thus worsened the patient's debility! It is easier for industrial countries to take advantage of a sick patient and that has actually happened in South Korea, Thailand and Indonesia.

Second, regardless of the hidden agendas of others, we must take further and urgent steps to reform our economy for our own sakes. If we do not do so, we will inadvertently play into the hands of those who have sinister designs or agendas of their own. Then, we will be forced to go to the IMF to bail us out (even if we are prepared to be poor, as Dr Mahathir Mohamad has reiterated) because international pressure and the need for our own economic survival will push us to go to the IMF!

We should, therefore, reform the National Development Policy and liberalise the Foreign Investment Guidelines immediately to make Malaysia much more competitive and resistant to the IMF agenda. We can do it judiciously according to our national interests and objectives, but we should not dilly-dally unduly.

Third, there is now a new emerging threat to our economic stability and recovery and this is the weakening federal government's Budget. We should not allow the Budget to deteriorate to a deficit, especially on the Budget's current account. Although the Budget's revenues will decline dramatically because of the economic slowdown, we have to make sure that we keep a strong surveillance over its operating expenditure. We have to bite the bullet even if it means cutting down on social expenditures, although this will be unfortunate. Perhaps defence expenditures should be further trimmed for the sake of agriculture, education and health services.

Fourth, we should refrain from borrowing too much to cover our projected overall Budget deficits. More so, we should not borrow to cover any deficits in the Budget's current account. If we do this, then it means that we are borrowing to pay the salaries of our civil servants. That will be most imprudent, as it will be inflationary. Similarly, it will also be undesirable to borrow excessively to finance the new asset management company.

It is thus gratifying that our civil servants and labour unions have shown much maturity and patience in restraining demands for wage increases. *Can you imagine the economic damage if our workers were militant like those in some other countries?*

In the end, we must aim for at least a balanced budget in our current account.

Fifth, we must ensure that we refrain from policies and practices that will undermine confidence in our capacity to manage our economy effectively. The rescue of corporates must be undertaken with care and savvy. We must give more priority and attention to minority interests in our corporates if we wish to avoid criticism and confusion over inadequate transparency in our transactions. If we take the line that if others can do it so can we, then we will have to face the consequences of low and slow foreign investment inflows. Unfortunately, the world as we know it is full of hypocrisy and double standards. If we can't beat the rich countries, we will apparently have to join them for our own good. At the same time, we will have to bargain hard to get the best deal for ourselves.

That is why we must resist the WTO from pushing us to give further concessions to the rich countries under the proposed new agenda in the new Millennium Round. While we have to liberalise, we cannot go too far or too fast, otherwise we will be unable to compete with the giants of the West. We need time to prepare ourselves for more liberalisation, and the West must understand our aspirations. Otherwise, there will be confrontations or conflicts between the rich and poor countries at some stage!

But to liberalise and globalise by gradually opening up more of our markets to foreigners, we will have to liberalise more internally at home. The IMF would surely want us to do so immediately, but we would rather liberalise internally over a longer period of time in a carefully planned and sensitive manner.

Regulations and controls that used to be much stricter in the past were rapidly lifted under the advice of international agencies that preached the virtues of free capital flows but neglected to warn about the dangers of erratic investor sentiments. Unplanned integration into the global economy and pursuit of liberalisation without thorough preparation and evaluation of strengths and capacity of national economies can unleash forces that can wipe away the gains of the past.

Reforming the NDP

Therefore, some of the more protective aspects of the NDP must be modified, if not removed, according to our own acceptable schedule. The reduction of internal protection will make us more competitive and competent in our management of the economy. We would also become even more competitive with our neighbours and even the industrial countries. We can reform and restructure on our own, without suffering the pain of doing so through the IMF. But we must reform, otherwise we are going to lose out to those countries that are now reforming and restructuring under the heartless IMF policies.

I suggest that we start modifying the NDP now on our own terms, rather than get into a situation where the IMF has to come in and dictate to us. That would be untenable because the IMF has shown that it has no soul. Its approaches are outdated and based on textbook theories that do not appreciate social, cultural and political realities.

Sixth, the need for greater public accountability and transparency in response to the economic downturn is all the more important now. The need for more transparency has been touted by the West about the East. However, what is important is the need for greater accountability. We could be more transparent and get to know what is going wrong, but if the perpetrators of wrongdoings are able to escape scot-free, then more transparency will mean just more frustration and a greater loss of credibility and confidence. Wrongdoers must be brought to book and made to pay for their misdemeanours. They must be made more accountable and answerable in their conduct.

The economic crisis in the Asian region has shown that greater transparency and accountability are imperative in managing the economies, particularly in the face of globalisation and liberalisation. *Although currency attacks by speculators had a direct impact on the Asian economies, rampant corruption, nepotism and cronyism had, to some extent, exacerbated the problem. But they were not the main reasons for the downturn.* After all, these negative elements are not confined to Asian countries alone. They are prevalent in developed nations as well—but they will not admit it!

In some countries, leaders who are guilty of wrongdoings, resign on their own volition. In some countries, they not only contemplate but commit suicide. But in Malaysia, they manage to escape the law and even live on to prosper later.

So, why is there a need to be professional, honest and disciplined? Why should one need to have a conscience when he is not made answerable or accountable for mismanagement? We have water shortages, brazen open burning, indiscriminate dumping of rubbish and toxic wastes, air and river pollution, and yet so few owners or managers have been made accountable. Hardly anyone resigns for mismanagement and only a few are sacked for misdemeanours. Some of those who fail in business get rescued. Their failures need not be entirely due to the decline in the value of the ringgit or share prices. In fact, their negligence, over-indulgence and incompetence could have initiated, if not largely caused, the collapse of the ringgit and the stockmarket.

Are we throwing good money after bad money? And where is this money coming from to rescue these bankrupt businesses?

There is a limit to the resources of Petronas, the EPF and certainly from the government's Budget. *Even if some of these scarce resources are used, will we be optimising on the allocation of our financial resources?* We would be misallocating our resources and thus causing damage to our credibility, confidence, economic recovery, long-term stability and progress, if we rescue companies that are badly managed or those that are not viable.

So, the first step in the long process of reform is to make all managers responsible and accountable to the people for their mismanagement. Those who have mismanaged government agencies or private companies must be punished. Unless we embark on a stronger culture of accountability, we will continue to tolerate inefficiencies that can erode our socio-economic and political systems. It could also jeopardise our aspirations for the attainment of the noble goals of Vision 2020. In fact, Dr Mahathir has already warned us that Vision 2020 may now be out of reach by the year 2020. He could well be right!

Seventh, we must have more confidence in our economy and its prospects for recovery. Apparently many Malaysian businessmen are transferring millions of ringgit overseas. This is reducing available liquidity in the banking system and putting more pressure on the government to raise interest rates.

If we send money abroad, we cannot at the same time expect our interest rates to go down. If our interest rates, though already high, go up further, then more businesses, big and small, will get into trouble. This will cause non-performing loans to rise and erode the banking system further.

In fact, some Singapore banks are offering much higher interest rates of about 20-30 per cent per annum for ringgit deposits. This is aggravating the outflow of ringgit and exacerbating the liquidity crunch in the country.

The solution would be to inculcate more confidence in Malaysians and to keep their funds at home. An estimated outflow of about RM20 billion is too high an amount to sustain. It is a tremendous drain on our low reserves and indeed on the whole economy. This will undermine confidence too. Needless to say, we must reduce this outflow.

But how do we encourage Malaysians to have more confidence in the Malaysian economy?

Businessmen, like everyone else, are driven by profits and will want to put their money where their mouths are. The higher interest earnings in Singapore will entice them to deposit their funds in Singapore so as to make more money.

There is apparently much anxiety over the viability of some of our banks. There is also concern that there could be constraints on sending money abroad if our liquidity gets tighter. Maybe there are some speculators who feel that the ringgit will appreciate soon. Hence, it is good to hoard more ringgit now to cash in for profit when it appreciates later. On the other hand, there is also the theory that currency speculators are buying the ringgit in order to dump them. Then they would buy back the ringgit for a song and then sell it later at a higher price. The high interest rates for ringgit deposits in Singapore could be due to speculators being short of ringgit. The currency market is a strange place and can be quite irrational as we well know. Currency traders are also very unscrupulous and have no qualms about the damage and poverty their actions may cause to developing countries.

Whatever the reasons, the problem of tight liquidity remains. The balance of payments is only improving slowly. But we need more liquidity in the system to prevent the economy from sliding into a recession. The only way out is to go all out to bring in foreign direct and equity investment. It is worth repeating here that we must relax our foreign investment guidelines soon if we are to prevent economic stagnation or, worst still, an impending recession.

Given the rising inflation and stagnation in the economy, we may soon have, as we did in the mid-1980s, a damaging stagflation in the economy. What we desperately need now are radical policies to increase confidence in the Malaysian economy as soon as possible before we slide into the abyss of stagflation.

Malaysia Incorporated

The private sector has gained considerably from the practice of Malaysia Incorporated, a "smart partnership" between government and business to enhance economic growth.

The implementation of this policy, however, has not always worked well. Some businessmen have exploited this policy to their selfish ends without concern for public interests. Of course, these businessmen cannot pursue their narrow interests without the tacit collaboration of some politicians and officials. After all, the authority to grant approvals comes from official sources. The link is quite obvious, but it is all done in the name of Malaysia Incorporated.

So, this is how Malaysia Incorporated can be abused. When businessmen and the authorities collaborate for their own vested interests, and not for the public good or national interests, then society suffers. It is thus important that the Malaysia Incorporated policy become more transparent to ensure that public interests are protected and preserved. This is the way to reduce cronyism and nepotism which is undeniably practised all over the world. We must improve our practices under Malaysia Incorporated.

Privatisation

Similarly, privatisation is a fine way of getting the private sector to be the engine of economic growth. It is supposed to bring greater benefits to society as it is presumed to provide more efficient services at more competitive prices to consumers.

But, unfortunately, there is growing concern that privatisation is providing less efficient services than government has provided in the past. Privatisation is also in many instances raising the cost of providing essential services to the consumer.

What causes lower quality of services for higher costs is the way some contracts are awarded? Very often the big contracts are privatised after negotiations rather than adopting the time-honoured practice of open tenders.

Unfortunately, and often enough, the wrong persons, without much experience, are given huge contracts that they cannot manage efficiently or competitively. The result is that there is much wastage of public funds. This causes strains on the balance of payments, the government's budget and the whole economy.

In the meantime, many people suffer and lose confidence not only in the privatisation policy but in the government's capacity to manage effectively. Some cynics have called privatisation by malicious names such "piratisation" and "personalisation".

It is thus essential that privatisation is conducted in a more transparent manner, especially in the awarding of tenders and contracts. They should be subject to more open competition so that the best contractor gets the job, regardless of his connections or influence. Some preference, of course, can be accorded to *Bumiputera* contractors in accordance with the NDP. But these concessions should not be unreasonable or excessive, otherwise there will be wastage that the taxpayers will have to pay for, in one form or another!

This is where it is vital that we do not mix business and policy. Privatised projects that are given out to political agents are likely to be the most costly, least efficient and most wasteful. The close proximity between business and politics goes against the grain of fair competition and fair pricing. Some politicians tend to be soft on the businessman involved in privatisation, especially when there is a deal that some of the profits will be given to the political party concerned or some politicians themselves!

The solution to this problem is to remove the preference given to politicians but to view the competition for privatisation, purely on technical and financial merits of the businessmen in their bids for contracts—with reasonable preference for only good and able *Bumiputera* contractors.

The IMF's Hidden Agenda

The IMF is failing the developing world. Our worst fears of its incompetence have been confirmed. The IMF has to take a significant responsibility for the socio-economic tragedies in Indonesia in May 1998.

One need not be a brilliant economist to know that you can't suddenly withdraw subsidies on basic essential commodities. This is exactly what the IMF insisted upon in Indonesia and thus caused prices of these essential commodities like kerosene and petrol to rise several times over! Naturally, the low-income groups reacted violently. *Would the IMF prescribe such policies in the industrial countries?*

Unfortunately, the IMF managing director showed the audacity of the IMF and its gross insensitivity when he responded that the IMF had expected the hard times in Indonesia resulting from IMF reforms. *What kind of economics does the IMF preach and practice if their proposals cause misery to millions of people?*

But the IMF and some of its major shareholders in the North would have done well and achieved their purpose, if their agenda was more reasonable and empathetic to the countries in the South. *Could the IMF been acting on the behest of powerful oligarchists in the West, more specifically in the United States?* The lesson to be learnt here is to avoid the IMF like the plague. But to do so, we will have to ensure that we are healthy.

But are we doing enough to accelerate our economic recovery and keep the IMF at bay? I am not sure. In fact, I believe we can do much more, unless we are prepared to limp along like a wounded tiger, instead of lunging forward as soon as possible. We need to heal the wounded tiger!

We need to lick our wounds quickly now, overcome our weaknesses and that of the external financial environment and gain economic strength as a matter of priority. Our leaders can show us the way forward through their determination and strong leadership. *This is a time of unprecedented complexity and uncertainty, a new era that is testing the skills of the world's most experienced leaders. The question is whether the leaders of the industrial world will rise to the occasion or fail us again?*

The G7 Agenda and the Role of Oligarchists

Considering the IMF's lacklustre track record, it is therefore most discouraging that the 1998 G7 Meeting of the richest industrial countries in the world has strongly supported the IMF's role in Asia. This is revealing as the IMF has now got Indonesia in the palm of its hand. Its policies and recommendations have directly contributed to the social upheavals and political instability in Indonesia, leading to the resignation of President Suharto in May 1998. Is this what the IMF and some of its major shareholders, who are also members of the G7, wanted in the first place. *Was the IMF their agent to pursue and achieve their hidden agenda?*

I sometimes wonder whether the G7 would have taken this cavalier stand if the IMF polices had caused severe social unrest in any country in the West? The G7 stand shows their indifference for the welfare of the South or ignorance of the damaging consequences of IMF policies in Indonesia and in other countries of the South.

The South should take this callous conduct of the G7 as a clear indication of the negative attitude of some of their members and an indication of some hidden agenda, which is to continue dominating the South. In time, the IMF and the WTO will be used as tools to subjugate the South. We have to be forewarned and therefore become more wary of the North, in general, and in particular some powerful industrial countries of the North, lead by the oligarchists in the United States!

Of course, some Western observers will dismiss this theory of a hidden agenda to dominate the South as pure rhetoric. But as we know, the proof of the pudding is in the eating. We have experienced time and again the underlying currents to undermine the long-term interests of the South countries. It started with the yoke of colonialism and has since then gone through various guises! Some call this new trend *new colonialism* or *recolonisation*.

While the West may see the currency crisis as a confirmation that free-market capitalism is the only viable financial system, there are others who believe the crisis to be a direct result of rapid globalisation and a Western conspiracy to stop the spectacular growth of Asian nations.

On our part, we must be more determined in resisting these strategic and stealthy efforts to subjugate and dominate developing countries. If we ignore these signs of the times, we do so at our own peril!

Asset Management Company

The establishment of an asset management company by the government will go long way towards raising confidence and promoting economic recovery. Modelled along the lines of similar organisations set up in the United States, Japan and Sweden, the asset management company aims to buy over the non-performing loans and assets of commercial banks at current market prices and selling them at a profit when prices recover.

The asset management company will acquire the non-performing loans and assets of banking institutions. The objective is to turn the business of borrowers into viable ventures so that the AMC would be able to sell them later as going concerns which will carry greater value.

The asset management company is not a bailout mechanism. By easing the burden of bad loans from the banks, the AMC will strive to turn around the banks that have to liquidate or sell their assets. The funding of the asset management company will come from the government, the private sector and through the issue of bonds and other debt instruments by the asset management company itself. Foreign investors are expected to be included in the ownership and management of the asset management company.

The asset management company could be a key factor in the recovery of the Malaysian economy. Banks should not waste their time and other resources on loan recovery at the expense of their productive capacity in seeking new borrowers to increase lending opportunities. The asset management company will have real expertise that can sell the acquired assets to those investors who have funds available.

One important source of keen buyers will be foreign investors. The prices of some local assets have declined by as much as 80 per cent if we take into account the depreciation of the ringgit as well as the fall in share prices and the drop in the value of properties.

This could be a bargain time for foreign investors, especially if the government relaxes its rules on foreign ownership. The present policy is to allow majority foreign ownership for foreign investors who export the bulk of their products. For instance, a foreign company that exports more than 80 per cent of its output is allowed even 100 per cent ownership of the company.

But what the asset management company should do is to obtain government permission to allow more than 50 per cent ownership for all foreign investors across the board, except for a few selected industries that affect defence and economic security.

The asset management company could then become the catalyst to bring together domestic and foreign investors, to take over some of the many companies that will be in trouble and slide during this economic slowdown. This way the slowdown could be arrested and the chances of a severe recession could be reduced. Economic recovery will then be more likely to take place as the rehabilitated companies begin to recover and add strength to the economy.

But there is always the fear that banks and financial institutions might treat the asset management company as a way to wipe their slates clean. Prudent safeguards must therefore be put in place to prevent the banks from abusing or exploiting the asset management company, by giving out loans to those who had previously defaulted on payments, on the understanding that the new asset management company will not bail them out for their continuing indiscretion!

Conclusion

We are now in a tight spot with not many choices and limited time. We have to choose the right strategy or a combination of strategies simultaneously and act with greater urgency, or face a severe recession. It would appear, at this time, that we are choosing economic strategies which will not ensure early economic recovery. Unless the National Economic Action Council (NEAC), a body established to oversee Malaysia's economic recovery, comes up with a package containing significant and urgent policy proposals, we may take more than two years to move out of a possible recession towards economic recovery.

We should thus not waste any more time by taking more courageous decisions to establish a greater sense of unity and adopt a more purposeful stance in managing an economy in crisis. The NEAC can spell the difference between the Malaysian economy moving into severe recession or beginning to stop the rot and moving out of a recession towards gradual economic renewal and recovery.

Chapter 2

RESTORING CONFIDENCE & STIMULATING RECOVERY

AT the 52nd Umno General Assembly on June 19-21, 1998, a suggestion was made that the government develop a social safety net for the low-income groups. Prime Minister and Umno President Dato' Seri Dr Mahathir Mohamad then assured Malaysians that "no one will be neglected or their problems glossed over by the government during these difficult economic times."

This is indeed a fine statement of government policy in handling the economic crisis. It is particularly reassuring to the people that they will not be forgotten, despite the considerable attention given to help the corporate sector. Those non-*Bumiputeras* who sometimes feel that they are relatively neglected by the government will also be encouraged as they would also be included in the social safety net. *How could they be left out?* It would be too obvious and politically embarrassing!

After all, it has to be constantly remembered that corporate leaders and big businesses are not the only or main source of economic strength. It is the humble men and women from all walks of life who form the backbone of the economy and they should not be taken for granted. Without their understanding and support our economy will stagnate and collapse—and political leaders will lose out!

But our fiscal and monetary policies now appear to be designed mainly to help the big corporates fight the recession. For this reason alone, Dr Mahathir's assurance is gratifying as obviously much more needs to be done for the people as they are already badly affected. They will be suffering even more than usual from the worsening economic situation. Retrenchment, unemployment, inflation and the inability to meet basic needs will hit the poor harder than the rich. That is why the poor must not be forgotten and be accorded higher priority in economic planning. Otherwise, they may also react from their suffering and rend the fabric of socio-economic stability.

What can be done to help the poor?

The fact is that Malaysia's resources are depleting and there are serious constraints to helping the poor at this time of economic slowdown.

The banking system is facing a liquidity crunch partly because of large capital outflows and the need to tighten monetary policy. Thus, interest rates are at an all-time high and businesses find it difficult to secure new loans, besides servicing their outstanding loans. They are unable to borrow enough to meet their needs. Their loans are being withdrawn, sometimes quite ruthlessly by financial institutions. Many companies are facing foreclosure by the banks.

Some foreign banks are particularly uncaring as they are dealing with foreigners who are Malaysians! They have been some of the first to pull the plug.

It is thus ironic that RM2.5 billion in loans are available to small-scale industries and for agricultural food production, but this has not been fully utilised. *Surely something can be done to help overcome this serious problem?*

Most entrepreneurs, especially the new *Bumiputera* business-men, are suffering from the tight monetary policy. The growing cry is to lower interest rates so as to reduce the debt burden of these companies. If these companies are saved, then the economy will recover faster.

According to former Deputy Prime Minister and Minister of Finance Dato' Seri Anwar Ibrahim, RM32 million had left the banking system since July 1997. Such a large outflow of capital is no doubt a cause for concern. *What are the possible causes of capital flight and what can we do to stem it?* The already disadvantaged exchange rate of the ringgit against the greenback may be further weakened if the outflow continues. If banking reserves go down, Bank Negara Malaysia may not have sufficient funds to fortify the ringgit, if required to do so.

The massive outflow of the ringgit is because of two reasons: first, foreign fund managers who hold money in the country either in the banking system or shares are withdrawing their money; and second, locals who send their money across the causeway or elsewhere due to the much higher interest rates offered. For instance, around June-July 1998, the interest rate was about 20-30 per cent for a one-month fixed deposit in Singapore compared to around 11 per cent in local banks.

Although the most immediate action to counteract the high interest rates overseas would be to match it, such a measure is inadvisable. When interest rates for deposits are increased, lending rates will automatically rise. This will worsen the situation as more debtors will not be able to pay off their loans. There will then be a more severe credit crunch.

The main reason people are taking money out of the country is because people are not sure when the economy is going to pick up. They think it is going to get worse before it gets better. The only thing that can be done to improve matters would be to take up more policymaking measures that will help build confidence in the nation's economy.

41

Monetary Policy

But the problem is that if we relax monetary policy too much and too soon, it can be damaging in the long term. Lowering interest rates too drastically, raising the lending limits to individual borrowers, and generally encouraging the growth of liquidity can have the following adverse implications on the economy.

Adverse Implications

First, confidence in the economy will worsen. Foreign analysts and investors, especially those influenced by the International Monetary Fund (IMF), may get the impression that we have lost our grip in steering the economy out of a possible recession.

Second, the ringgit could depreciate further, despite the present strengthening of the balance of payments. The financial analysts and speculators will bet on the ringgit, weakening the currency further. All this would invite further attacks on the ringgit and cause the ringgit to be even more unstable.

Third, lower interest rates, more liquidity and a weakening ringgit could put even more pressure on the worsening inflationary situation.

In the end, the poor will suffer most from rising prices, especially for food and other basic items. *Thus, if there are serious limitations to using monetary policies to help the poor and the economy to recover, where can we go for help?*

Borrowing

Declining revenue and the impossibility of further expenditure cutbacks will not generate enough surplus and public savings to increase investment to counter the economic slowdown. But there is a way out. Malaysia could borrow more to assist the businessmen and the poor who have been adversely affected by the economic slowdown. But there are problems and risks in borrowing too much.

It is argued that since Malaysia's external debt servicing is still relatively low at around 6 per cent of export earnings and since domestic debt servicing is only about 14 per cent of the Budget expenditure, we can safely borrow more.

This argument is acceptable but is also fraught with weaknesses and concerns such as the following:

First, more borrowing would be the easiest way out. *But is it the safest option?* We should be careful not to be seen as wanting to borrow ourselves out of a recession.

Second, there are also severe limits as to how much we can borrow. The more we borrow from abroad, the more indebted and beholden we will be to foreign lenders and foreign interests.

Third, unless foreign borrowing is linked to specific projects, such as required by World Bank loans, there is a danger that general foreign market borrowing could be used to finance non-viable, low-priority projects and programmes. Thus, the ability to repay such loans will become questionable.

Domestic borrowing by the government through government securities and even bonds will also raise the debt burden. However, this is acceptable particularly if the loans are meant to promote economic growth. The additional RM7 billion for development and RM5 billion for critical infrastructure projects are thus most welcomed. Mild reflation is now necessary.

But if we raise our debt to finance an asset management company, then there is minimal promotion of economic growth and income distribution, although it will help strengthen the banking system and the corporate sector.

The poor will not benefit unless this new domestic borrowing is used to promote small-scale agriculture and SMIs to a larger extent.

We must be careful that we do not divert scarce resources that we borrowed to rescue the rich while the poor suffer. We need to maintain a balance in resource allocation.

What the asset management company will be doing is nevertheless useful: by buying good assets pledged to the banks, it will be able to help turn around weak companies to make them more viable and their assets more productive and profitable.

Foreign Capital

However, given these monetary and budgetary limitations, the best boost to the economy may come from the inflow of new foreign capital that could buy these bank assets that are taken over by the AMC. The asset management company could provide the much-needed boost for banks drowned with bad loans, only if it plays its role effectively. It must not just be a liquidity provider but must be able to rehabilitate bad loans in an independent and judicious manner, regardless of who owns the assets.

The challenge to the asset management company then would be to bring in foreign capital that can work with Malaysian capital, to own and operate Malaysian companies much more efficiently and profitably—with more transparency and competence as the basis for good governance. But we must remember that the asset management company alone cannot be depended upon to solve all the problems of the banks, some of which the banks created themselves through their own inefficiencies and incompetencies. We will therefore need to open up even more to greater foreign participation in the Malaysian economy and in banking and finance, on a selective basis, in order to recover more rapidly.

We need to bring in more foreign capital and technological and management competence to carefully selected areas of our economy. This is the best way in the short term to quickly improve the quality and competitiveness of our business culture and governance so as to aid economic recovery. Of course, foreign investment is not going to come into Malaysia just because we want it to. According to the United Nations Conference on Trade and Development (UNCTAD), foreign investment is now going to comparatively more attractive countries in Latin America and the Caribbean and central and eastern Europe which had lost out in the past to Asia. The tide has turned against us. Foreign investment is moving out to other regions.

FDI and Bumiputera Ownership

Minister of Trade and Industry Dato' Seri Rafidah Aziz has stated that we received only 212 applications valued at about RM4.027 billion in the first four months of 1998. These figures indicate that there will be a decline in foreign investment in 1998 as compared to 1997. This is the perhaps the reason why she has also stated that the "government is fine-tuning some policies regarding foreign-equity structure, incentives and costs". This initiative is most timely and could help pull us out of possible stagflation and even a long drawn-out recession. We need to move imaginatively and innovatively to emerge from this economic crisis quickly. I suggest that foreign investors be given more than 51 per cent ownership and that about 30 per cent to be reserved for *Bumiputeras*, while the remainder could be kept for non-*Bumiputeras*, at least for all the investors who invest in the next five years. After all, the Umno General Assembly also encouraged long-term foreign investment in selected areas, including banking and finance!

Since the commanding heights of the economy are already in *Bumiputera* hands and since the whole government *machinery* is managed essentially by *Bumiputeras*, it is time to relax the NDP and to liberalise the economy from excessive restrictions and controls. Such controls often create fertile ground for the festering of cronyism and corruption and internal capitalistic abuse, just as unfettered foreign capital can exploit our economy, if left unchecked.

Managing Market Forces and Conspiracies

But given the existing international economic and financial system where the West controls the levers of power, what can we do? What are the options opened to us?

First, it may be incorrect to lump all industrial countries as the exploitative and avaricious West. There are indeed some Western governments that are more enlightened and insightful of the longer-term dangers to themselves, of continuing domination of the South. History is full of instances of oppressed countries' reactions and the retribution against the oppressors.

Second, we need to identify and collaborate with all fair-minded governments, NGOs and individuals in the West who see the need for more just economic policies in the longer-term interests of world stability and peace. Like-minded groups can change policies within their governments in alliance with those from all over the world. We must not think that all industrial countries are like the rich and powerful oligarchists in the United States government.

Third, we have to separate avaricious capitalists and selfish currency manipulators from governments and countries, both in the West and in the South or East as well. We should not always link greedy oligopolists or monopolists who crave exorbitant profits at the expense of human welfare to all Western governments. If we do so, then we are suggesting that there is a worldwide conspiracy to suppress the South. This is not plausible because it is difficult to obtain that degree of consensus and secrecy in organising such an evil conspiracy on a worldwide basis.

It is possible, however, that excessively greedy capitalists, oligarchists and oligopolists could be united in their common cause, to squeeze every pound of profits, even without having to conspire. That is the culture of avaricious capitalists. This is also the basis for the invisible hand of conspiracy against the South—to keep them down! But those guilty Westerners will dismiss this charge as rhetorical!

Fourth, it is therefore imperative to seek a New International Order that will regulate and discipline the conduct of these huge multinational oligarchists. Then we could reduce the degree of economic exploitation and curtail their power to dominate the peoples and governments of the South (or even the North). After all, according to Prof J.K. Galbraith, the power and influence exercised by the industrial military complex in the United States is overwhelming and frightening. It is indeed difficult for ex-colonialists to change their mindsets. After all, leopards cannot change their spots.

Finally, we must accept the realty of the capitalist system and the presence and power of market forces. We should not, as Dr Mahathir says "submit to market forces". Therefore, we need to be alert to their signals and make adjustments in order to avert the disruptive effects of market forces. *We need to build up our economic strength and institutions and push for higher levels of good governance to resist the rapacious and avaricious forces of both naked and neo-capitalism.*

That is why we have to carry on fighting against corruption, nepotism and crony capitalism. At the same time, we must lead in the campaign to bring about genuine reforms in the outdated international monetary system.

International Monetary Reform

While we take steps to improve our internal governance, we should ensure that currency manipulators do not destroy all that we have built up over the last four decades since independence in 1957. It is no use achieving a high level of good governance in the government and business sectors, if currency manipulators shatter our successes as they like from time to time. The IMF reports and proposed reforms of the international monetary system will therefore be awaited with keen interest. But the IMF, because it is largely owned and managed by vested interests in the United States and other major Western countries, is likely to drag its feet. *What we desperately need is an IMF that does not represent the interest of any cause or any country, but to bridge the gap between the developed and developing world.*

Malaysia and other like-minded countries in the South (and even in the North) must therefore begin introducing their own regulatory policies to minimise the dangers and damage caused by huge speculative short-term capital movements.

Thus, the Commonwealth Expert Group's recent study on how to manage volatile short-term capital flows could be adopted by Malaysia as early as possible where appropriate.

The tentative recommendations are as follows:

First, introduce "standstill mechanisms" for recipient countries to control the outflow of capital in case of crisis.

Second, negotiate with private creditors for orderly resettlement of foreign debt with the help of the IMF. The IMF is expected to play a more positive role in making the rich lenders to be responsible for "moral hazards". So far they have got away scot-free while the poor borrowers have been severely penalised.

Third, both lenders and borrowers must bear the burden of losses due to a currency crisis. So far the foreign lenders have insisted on their debt settlement although they were partly to blame for persuading borrowers to borrow imprudently.

Fourth, in addition, some tax or disincentives could also be introduced to discourage volatility in the capital market.

Fifth, Bank Negara Malaysia could develop an early-warning system to trigger concern and controls when speculative short-term capital movements reach critical levels.

The government could adopt some of these measures to better manage large, volatile movements of short-tern capital flows as soon as possible.

UMNO General Assembly 1998:
Economic Implications

The 1998 UMNO General Assembly reflected a great deal maturity and provided pertinent guidelines to the government for the management of the current economic crisis. The resolutions on economic management were positive, prudent and sufficiently broad to enable the government to use its discretion in the actual design and implementation of new strategies, as follows:

First, the government will have to continue giving priority to the promotion of *Bumiputera* interests. The NDP will not necessarily be slowed down to achieve faster rates of growth and economic recovery. The rescue of *Bumiputera* companies and the subsidies for essential commodities will continue.

Second, there will be further relaxation in the tight monetary policies adopted so far.

Third, the IMF-type economic crisis management policies will be kept further at bay, as we will depend on our own savings within and outside the country, to step up our investments. Instead, Malaysia may go to the World Bank instead of the IMF for help.

Fourth, the government, however, will be allowed to attract more long-term investment capital on a broader but selective basis, provided the *Bumiputera* share is protected. *This could mean that the 51 per cent ownership desired by most large foreign investors would be granted more liberally.*

Fifth, the government is encouraged to be more transparent in its transactions and policies. This would reduce corruption and any nepotism. Thus it is clear that Malaysia will continue to adopt its own strategies to overcome the economic crisis without taking drastic measures. Consequently, we will be more stable. Though it is arguable whether the economy will take longer to recover as a result of pursuing gradual rather than radical measures.

Cronyism

The issue of cronyism was discussed at length during the UMNO General Assembly. Cronyism can be regarded as the practice of associating closely with influential leaders and gaining undue concessions through the relationship. The concessions can be in the form of favors of all kinds. These can be mainly large contracts and privileged licences which lead to monopolies and oligopolies and often inordinately large profits.

Those who gain concessions because of official government polices to help the disadvantaged and the poor cannot be regarded as cronies. What they receive are small concessions which is their legitimate right as deserving citizens who need special attention because of their disadvantaged position.

Even if the so-called cronies gained unfair profits, people generally will not mind so much if these concessions are not unduly large. What people object to and even resent are the huge concessions that are given to some few selected individuals. The revulsion is stronger when these excessive concessions are given to individuals who are inexperienced new businessmen who just collect rents and become the *nouveau riche*. Even these new rich will be excused if not for the fact that they become unreasonably rich without working hard or acquiring much business acumen! These cronies constitute the "rentier class". But there may not be many.

The words "nepotism" and "corruption" have been bandied about extensively in recent times, to describe the causes of the economic turmoil in Asia. The Western press has particularly found these terms useful in discrediting the Asian values of societal responsibility, filial piety, diligence and high thrift and savings, that economists have attributed as reasons for the much-vaunted Asian Miracle.

Asian Values

And now that the Asian economies have been badly hit by currency speculators and manipulators who took advantage of our economic weaknesses, some Western analysts and the mass media have come down with a vengeance to put Asian values and Asian countries down in order to highlight their own so-called superior Western value systems. This strategy is seen on CNN International and, particularly, CNBC Asia, where they try their best to enhance Western values and sneer at Eastern values in business and politics!

That is the general Asian perception of the Western bias towards Asia, Indeed that is the general perception of the South (poor ex-colonies) of the North (rich ex-colonialists).

But I believe that the perception of many Western analysts about crony capitalism is not entirely without foundation. After all, they know because they themselves have gone through the phase of crony capitalism in their own economic evolution. In many cases they are still practising it, as in the case of US President Bill Clinton and his Vice-President Al Gore and campaign funds.

Crony capitalism thrives in an environment of relative inexperience in democratic practices and when the traditional democratic institutions are weak. The informed and enlightened exercise of the vote, the independence of the judiciary, the professionalism of businessmen, civil servants, and the level of integrity of political leaders, as well as the impartial role of the mass media, are but some institutions that have to be well established before the abuses of democracy-like crony capitalism and corruption can be adequately controlled.

In the South, these democratic institutions are not very strong and sometimes even frail. But, worse still, these institutions may not even exist in their genuine form in some countries. Very often these institutions are non-existent or mere frameworks and a shadow of what they should be—largely because they were not established strongly by the colonialists.

Hence, it is fair to say that Asia and the South at their present stage of evolution have more scope for the practice of crony capitalism than the more sophisticated rich countries of the North. There are some who would even argue that if there is a choice between crony capitalism and economic growth, on the one hand, and more poverty, on the other, the choice would be to go for economic growth even if it includes cronyism, at least until countries in the South become more sophisticated.

It is, of course, better to have a mixture of capitalism and socialism and better governance so that there is steady economic growth with equity and stability. But that is the ideal which all societies should work towards. However, emerging economies need time to learn and mature into more sophisticated societies.

Malaysia has reached the stage, after 40 years of enviable progress since independence in 1957, to fight crony capitalism much more effectively. Crony capitalism, however, is not necessarily found only developing countries. It is prevalent in the rich developed countries too, but perhaps on a reduced scale. This is because they usually have a lively democracy and a more robust and alert press and opposition than those we find in most developing countries in the South.

There are also more active NGOs in the North that make it more difficult for cronyism to thrive in the developed countries. These NGOs are also vigilant against abuses within their own rich countries. The NGOs in developing countries therefore should be more active despite some constraints.

Recolonisation

Dr Mahathir has also argued persuasively that currency attacks will not cease until the country is again recolonised. I too subscribe to the theory that since the colonial era, most industrial countries in the North have sought to dominate the developing countries in the South through economic means and not military might or open political manipulation. How else could 20 per cent of the world's population control 80 per cent of the world's wealth. This is bullying and exploitation which we all have to change or face another world war sometime in the future!

However, there is not much we can do to revitalise the Malaysian economy immediately and to wipe out abuses. But the greater capital inflow into the Malaysian economy through more relaxed economic policies and management will stimulate economic recovery and enable the government to do more for the poor as well as the badly affected businessmen.

At the same time, the abuses of an excessively materialistic and capitalistic system could be minimised by better managed internal and global competition and the provision of more priority for a higher quality of life and a more caring society for the poor and unfortunate in Malaysia.

But we cannot discount the fact that we need more changes in government policy and priorities to help change the outlook for the poor as well as to improve the prospects of the economy.

Tun Daim Zainuddin

The appointment of Tun Daim Zainuddin as both Minister of Special Functions in charge of economic development and executive director of the NEAC is significant for the successful management of the Malaysian economy.

Why was this major move made? I will not get into the political implications as they are not very clear and also subject to all kinds of political speculation. What is more relevant and topical is to examine the implications of Tun Daim's appointment in getting Malaysia out of the recession and onto the road of economic recovery.

According to Dr Mahathir, Tun Daim will be able to present his views as chief executive of the NEAC more effectively in the Cabinet, now that he a full minister. In the past, his views were transmitted to Cabinet for discussion and decision. However, several ministers did not take well to many of the NEAC recommendations. They probably considered Tun Daim as interfering with their responsibilities and management. Some may even have considered Tun Daim of taking over their functions and posing a threat to their government positions and political futures.

Thus, under these circumstances, it would have been difficult for Dr Mahathir to get consensus to decide firmly on the recommendations of the NEAC. Even if decisions were made, it would have been difficult to implement these decisions effectively if there was no wholehearted and full support for the recommendations of the NEAC.

I believe it was for these reasons that Dr Mahathir decided to bring Tun Daim into the Cabinet. But now the question remains as to how the new arrangement is going to work. Tun Daim will be functioning as the new economic adviser with Cabinet rank. As minister responsible for economic affairs, he will have responsibility for dealing and even supervising the work of the Treasury, the Economic Planning Unit (EPU), the Ministry of Trade and Industry and Bank Negara Malaysia. All these agencies have a direct bearing on economic management and Tun Daim will undoubtedly exercise his influence and leadership over these agencies.

Whatever the dynamics of leadership in this new scenario, where the public is concerned, they will only want to see effective results. A major advantage is that it will be possible, with Dr Mahathir's backing of Tun Daim, and his complete trust in him, that decisions will now be made faster.

But only time will tell whether the inclusion of Tun Daim in the Cabinet will lead Malaysia out of the recession towards economic recovery faster, or whether the possible conflict and confusion will lead to greater uncertainty, lack of confidence and a longer-term recession and slower recovery.

Conclusion

We can help the poor as well as the business community during the economic crisis only if we stimulate economic recovery rapidly. This can be done through an attractive package of incentives to encourage more foreign investment and some limited borrowing and gradually lowering interest rates.

And now that Tun Daim, the executive director of the NEAC, is in the Cabinet, it is hoped that there will be more comprehensive and concerted policies in preventing a severe recession. We have high expectations for significant policy initiatives.

Chapter 3

INTEREST-RATE IMBROGLIO: A HIGH OR LOW REGIME?

IT is indeed reassuring that the National Economic Recovery Plan (NERP) has finally been made public. Public confidence has been raised by Dr Mahathir Mohamad's announcement that his Cabinet has decided to accept all the recommendations made by the NERP.

Besides being a realistic assessment of the state of health of the Malaysian economy, the NERP recommends a slew of pragmatic measures to address the economic and financial problems.

Hopes and expectations have now been strengthened that Malaysia will move more steadily out of recession towards economic recovery by the end of 1999. However, the public will not be whole-heartedly enthusiastic about these new proposals for economic recovery until they see real action for change, growth and stability.

Many of these NERP policies are general aims and aspirations at this juncture. *What are the specific measures and how much will they be effectively implemented? How long will it take and how good will these proposals be to pull us out of the recession?*

The real test of the pudding is in the eating. We will need to do much more homework to put these policy aims into action. This takes time and gives much cause for concern.

The NERP's most positive radical recommendation has been to allow 51 per cent foreign ownership in the manufacturing sector for approvals given up to December 31, 1999. This move is most encouraging as it will attract more foreign direct investment into the country. It will also placate foreign investors and raise their confidence as they have been eager to open up the Malaysian economy for their own benefit. But we may have to extend the deadline if insufficient foreign investment is forthcoming during this short duration of about 17 months.

Omissions

However, the glaring omissions in the NERP have been the neglect in the revision of the Industrial Coordination Act 1975. The present ceiling of RM2.5 million could have been raised to at least RM5 million to enable non-*Bumiputera* family and small businesses to expand without having to restructure and sell 30 per cent of their share capital to *Bumiputeras*.

This omission would continue to restrain and depress the SMIs which constitute the backbone of the domestic manufacturing sector. Any relaxation of these restrictions should be given as much publicity as possible. Otherwise, there will be no benefits from policy changes, if the SMIs are not aware of these policy changes.

The other omission is the absence of any proposal to reform the civil service. Thus, an important opportunity has been lost to make the civil service even more effective in actually implementing the many good proposals of the NEAC.

Civil service reform should also be addressed. There should be more decentralisation in decision-making. Too much power is still centralised in the Treasury and the Public Service Department (PSD). Therefore, other ministries and government agencies feel constrained and too rigidly controlled by the Treasury and the PSD. There must be more delegation to enable managers to do what they are supposed to do: manage.

Concerns

Concerns plaguing the public are as follows:

First, we must not wait for the 1999 Budget in October 1998 to change the laws and regulations governing the policies formulated in the NERP. We cannot afford to wait; we need to act urgently and decisively for optimal results.

Second, will the monitoring system announced by former Deputy Prime Minister and Minister of Finance Anwar Ibrahim be given enough powers to pull up and if necessary penalise the individuals and agencies that drag their feet in the implementation of the NERP proposals? They must be made to understand that there is need for a sense of urgency. If not, the implementation of the NERP will suffer.

Third, will the government fully report to the public on a weekly basis on the progress made in implementing these new policies and why they can or cannot be implemented expeditiously? We will need more open governance.

Fourth, unless a transparent schedule of target dates and achievements are made frequently and publicly, the new expectations and confidence in the NERP will gradually decline and diminish. This kind of development will then be most unfortunate as not only emotional but economic depression can set in. But we need to keep our hopes high. There is always hope even in bad times.

Fifth, borrowing. Initially about RM30 billion will need to be raised to stimulate the economy, to recapitalise the banking system and to handle the rising non-performing loans through an asset management company. But the sooner we are able to assess the full requirements, the easier it will be to plan effectively on how much we need to borrow and the sources of borrowing.

Now that two international rating agencies, Moody's Investors Service and Standard & Poor's (S&P's), have downgraded our sovereign risk rating due to the economic downturn, our foreign borrowing is going to cost very much more. Though such downgrading of credit-worthiness tend to heighten the sense of crisis, we must be cautious of such ratings because they have dubious ways of making decisions. If these rating agencies are seen to be following the herd instinct, rather than leading in sound analysis, then it is time for the agencies themselves to be assessed.

However, Thomson BankWatch, the world's largest bank rating agency, believes that Malaysia's NERP, by outlining a multi-faceted approach towards economic recovery, suggests that Malaysia is firming up its response to both the structural and cyclical aspects of the current downturn. If fully implemented, the NERP is likely to bolster the country's economic fundamentals over the longer term.

Thomson Bankwatch, part of the New York-based Thomson Financial Services Company, also said that Malaysia has demonstrated a strong track record of economic policy management over the past 15 years. This has endowed the economy with stronger fundamentals compared with some of its regional neighbours. Both foreign debt and the debt-servicing costs remain low and the proportion of short-term maturities remains manageable. Besides, Malaysia's efforts to modernise its economy and diversify its export mix would provide the country with a cushion to withstand periods of economic downturn.

The factors that led to the credit downgrading include the ongoing financial market volatilities, higher domestic debts and problems in the domestic banking and corporate sectors. Malaysia appeared to have become the latest victim of the ongoing Asian turmoil and depressed Asian outlook for trade and investment. The closely interlinked nature of regional economies, which had served to be a mutually supporting asset inflation during boom times, is now proving to be a liability, particularly for stronger economies like Malaysia.

We must keep our rising debt in check. It is just as well there-fore that the government has postponed the issue of bonds.

Sixth, we will also have to be very careful in choosing the pro-jects and companies that would need financial help. Both foreign in-vestors and the Malaysian public will have to wait and see if these projects and companies are viable and strategic and that helping them will indeed be in the public and national interests.

The confidence that is now building up has to be meticulously maintained, strengthened and sustained. Otherwise, our efforts at rebuilding confidence will be wasted.

Seventh, if we ascribe undue blame on external economic forces for our economic decline, then we could be distracted from what we should do to help ourselves. We will need to cultivate our foreign friends. We must remember that we have many good friends and supporters in the West. We must not tar all countries in the West with the same brush. We must desist from labelling all coun-tries and individuals in the West as bad. There are many Western governments and people who are fair-minded, scrupulous and sym-pathetic to the emerging economies and other poor countries.

Eighth, in the meantime, it is worrisome that the United States and some other rich countries are allowing the IMF (if not encour-aging) to delay action on the proposed reforms of the international monetary system.

It has been more than a year since Dr Mahathir called for bet-ter discipline, transparency and management of the destructive massive movements of short-term funds. But hardly anything has happened in the interim. Perhaps when the enlarging New York Stock Exchange (NYSE) bubble actually bursts, then the mighty United States might show some positive leadership. By then it may be too late!

The Role of the United States

At the same time, the United States Secretary of State Madeleine Albright has recently called on the East Asian nations to take more of the "bitter medicine" that has been prescribed by the International Monetary Fund.

The IMF has already been seriously discredited by its less-than-glowing track record and standard policies in Asia and elsewhere, and even by prominent Western economists and thinkers such as former US Secretary of State Dr Henry A. Kissinger. Nevertheless, Albright is singing the same old tune. Worse still, she does not even refer to the United States' responsibility and dismal record in hardly doing anything to protect weak defenceless Third World countries against the onslaught of currency attacks. Instead, the United States continues to pass the buck to Japan. So much for US diplomacy and fairness to the South! Japan can contribute by reflating its economy and building up its economy, but all its efforts will come to nought if the United States does not mean what it says. The United States needs to adopt a strong leadership role in introducing rapid reforms to the international monetary structure.

It is indeed debilitating to fight against domination, but we have no alternative but to soldier on! What the United States need to do is to reform and settle its massive debt to the United Nations and its IMF obligations as well. But the United States, I suppose, is entitled to practise double standards!

IMF Impact

A little over a year after the economic turmoil, we are thankful that we did not call in the IMF or use the full IMF dosage. If the IMF had come to Malaysia we could have had the following implications on our economy:

First, taxes would be increased.

Second, expenditures would have been cut down drastically, that is beyond the 18 per cent reduction in the government Budget.

Third, foreign borrowing would have been severely curtailed, except from the IMF itself, with all its crippling conditions.

Fourth, the Malaysian economy would have been forced open, for the benefit of foreign investors to come in and completely take over (or "*gobble-ise*" through globalisation) our major assets, even in the most sensitive areas like banking.

Fifth, many of our large and critical *Bumiputera* corporates would have been bought over at cheap fire-sale prices, as has happened in IMF-financed countries.

Sixth, our SMIs would have been denied soft loans and government support, and most of the weak *Bumiputera* SMIs in particular would have collapsed like a house of cards.

Seventh, vital subsidies for essential goods like rice, cooking oil, sugar, housing, etc would have been cut back or removed. There were riots in some IMF-financed countries over the withdrawal of these kinds of subsidies, and it could have happened here too.

Eighth, the National Development Policy would have been eroded by the IMF with all its serious social disruptions.

Ninth, inflation would have risen and social upheavals like in some of those IMF client countries could have occurred.

Lastly, the so-called US Treasury/IMF-WTO Axis would have prevailed and won the day! They would have succeeded in spreading their undue influence and dominance over yet another developing country.

Conspiracy

For all these to happen, there need not be a formal conspiracy. It could just be the informal uncoordinated movement of like-minded international socio-economic and political forces by the "invisible hand" that seeks profit at any price, regardless of the socio-economic and political damage it leave in its wake! If this "invisible hand" is also governed by like-minded ex-colonialists, committed to continued domination by some powerful industrial countries, then the suppression of the rights of developing countries becomes even more severe. This suppression would deny community and national human rights—but that is a different matter! The West, in more ways than one, is more interested in individual human rights!

But we have gone along (not with the IMF) with some universal fiscal and monetary measures to stabilise our economy. We have left out some of the destructive measures that the IMF would recommend as a matter of their routine standard practice.

Malaysianomics

Instead, we have been pragmatic and adopted economic measures that are better suited to our socio-economic and political environment. We have introduced and adopted "Malaysianomics". We have done it the Malaysian way, that is in our own national interests. Our aim has been to achieve economic recovery through the preservation of the sovereign commitment to national unity and social stability. In Malaysia's complex multiracial, multicultural milieu, the IMF's standardised and insensitive prescriptions can cause more harm than good. Indeed, it could cause disunity and disaster. Then no one else will suffer but Malaysians. Outsiders would comfortably remain on the sidelines and watch our troubles on CNN International or CNBC Asia in the comfort of their homes—and with glee by some.

Tougher Action

However, this does not necessarily mean that we can be soft in tackling our problems. We will have to be more determined and decisive in introducing internal changes.

For instance, the wide range of proposals presented during the Budget Dialogue will have to be implemented not only after the annual Budget in October of every year, but *urgently* and *there and then*. Similarly, the NEAC Report prescribed by the Minister of Special

Functions Daim Zainuddin will need to be acted upon with greater urgency.

The Financing Challenge

The real challenge in economic management to bring about economic recovery will be the government's ability to raise these large funds at reasonable cost, both in the short and long term. *Will the initial RM30 billion come from the EPF, Petronas, the Pilgrimage Fund Board (Lembaga Tabung Haji), the flotation of bonds or borrowing? Is the bulk of our funding to come from domestic or foreign sources?*

These are going to be the major issues for consideration and public debate in the next few months.

After all, more borrowing means the creation of more debt for posterity. It is our children and their children who will have to bear the burden of settling the debt, long after most of the older generation are gone. But there is no alternative unless this potential debt burden is reduced by encouraging more foreign investment to come in through greater liberalisation.

However, there still seems to be serious reservations about liberalising foreign ownership.

I believe if it is difficult to borrow these large sums, which could increase to RM40 billion or more, then the authorities may have to relax the rules on foreign direct investment.

In the meantime, we will have to wait and see how successful we will be in borrowing this huge amount. And then we will come back to the question of foreign confidence in our capacity to manage our economy with adequate efficiency. But for now, enough has been done to counter the recession. While it is felt that much more could have been done earlier to arrest the economic decline, it is nevertheless better late than never.

The Civil Service

While I will not comment on the efficacy of the Legislative and the Judiciary, I think I have some competence to consider the Malaysian civil service.

Dr Mahathir has suggested that the civil service should be revamped to overcome the current economic crisis. He should find much public support for his clarion call which has been long overdue. However, it is not only the civil service that needs to be revamped. It is the policies, rules and regulations that need to be reviewed and revised as matter of urgency. This in turn will enable more efficient administration by the civil service.

The inefficiencies in the civil service and the delays in approvals will carry on as along as there are so many regulations that have to be complied with, before any approval can be granted. A classic example is found in the low and medium housing and construction industry, where the approval process is tedious and cumbersome. It is no wonder that the poor are denied adequate housing and that investors are reluctant to invest in the housing industry. The delays in approvals at so many levels adds considerably to the cost of borrowing and financing in the housing and construction industries.

We have also too much politics in business and this is a major reason for slow approvals and the steady loss in our competitive position. Civil servants should be encouraged to be more professional in their work approach and less politically inspired.

Reasons for revamp of civil service

There are many reasons why the civil service has become slower and less effective. The main reasons are as follows:

First, we are not getting the better quality staff into the civil service, especially at the lower levels. Today, unlike in the past, one would tend to join the civil service at the lower levels, only if you can't get a better job elsewhere. This is because the salaries have become increasingly unattractive and the role of the civil service has been downgraded by the leaders over the years.

Second, unlike the private sector where you can be penalised or fired for inefficiency, the civil service in comparison tolerates weak officers. The really bad ones go into cold storage but they cause major morale problems. Nevertheless, unless civil servants are dishonesty, they continue to enjoy security of tenure. *So why work too hard and for long hours when you can survive with mediocrity? Disciplinary action itself takes a long time to administer, so why worry?* That, unfortunately, is the growing attitude amongst many civil servants today.

Third, the civil service does not adequately reflect the ethnic composition of the Malaysian society. Hence, there is lot of inbreeding which does not make it sufficiently competitive. It would be more efficient if it was more heterogeneous—like the Malaysian society. Then it would be easier to impose more discipline.

Fourth, the civil service is generally far too centralised, Most major policies governing service and establishment policies and principles are controlled by the Public Service Department (PSD). On the other hand, all major approvals of a financial nature are referred to the Treasury. Furthermore, economic development issues are invariably controlled by the Economic Planning Unit in the Prime Minister's Department. Hence, the delays in approvals when the system does not delegate enough.

The situation is further aggravated by the thirteen state governments that wield power over all land matters. They may obstruct or stifle economic development, intentionally or otherwise, simply by delaying land alienation approvals!

It is indeed a wonder therefore that we have progressed so far in socio-economic and political development, considering the cumbersome system of management.

Fifth, there is the underlying concern that approvals should only be given greater urgency if the approvals are in full compliance with the aspirations of the NDP. It is therefore sometimes regarded as only right and proper that decisions should be delayed, postponed or even rejected because they do not meet NDP requirements. This would not be regarded as procrastination or inefficiency but as expedient for some approving authorities and overzealous individuals. This attitude causes delays but it should not be confused by the private sector as inefficiency in the civil service.

However, thank goodness we still have a large number of dedicated civil servants in the MCS and the professions at the higher levels. But their numbers are declining. The staff at the lower levels of the public service are unfortunately far less competitive, compared to their more carefully selected counterparts in the private sector where they can be hired and fired much more readily. *So how can these lower-level unenthusiastic civil servants adequately serve the business and the public interests more efficiently?*

I believe that Dr Mahathir's call for a more hardworking and efficient civil service must be followed up with the establishment of a Civil Service Commission that could make recommendations to revamp and improve the civil service to serve Malaysia more efficiently to meet the challenges not only of our current socio-economic crisis, but especially the challenges of the 21st century.

I believe that if we do not act urgently to revamp the civil service, Dr Mahathir's courageous call for a more efficient civil service will be lost for a long time to come, to the detriment of our national progress.

To lower or not to lower interest rates

For the NERP to succeed, an accompanied easing of monetary policy is essential. According to Patrick Er, an economist with CIMB Securities, in his paper, "Malaysian monetary policy revisited: why interest rates need to come down now": "Easier monetary conditions now would be of tremendous immediate benefit to the economy in the sense that the preservation of the financial system and the industrial backbone is not compromised while the more arduous task of restructuring and reform is given 'breathing space' to take place." Furthermore, CIMB's econometric research also shows that regional currency movements are more important in influencing ringgit changes than interest rate differentials.

We must not be confused by the measures propagated and implemented by the IMF as part of their bailout package for troubled economies. As a rule of thumb, there is indeed no harm discussing prudent management, transparency and full disclosure. But we must not be deceived into believing that these "cookie-cutter" or "one-size-fits-all" measures must be implemented at all costs without comprehending the peculiarities of each society. For instance, why should poor economies be expected to adopt these measures while others are absolved from them. According to former Minister of Finance Anwar Ibrahim, "The IMF doesn't understand the complexities of each country but just hammers down these conditions." Up to July 1997, the World Bank had called East Asia the economic powerhouse of the century, but this "period of exuberance and optimism" has now been replaced by pessimism and a notion that "everything is disastrous and wrong".

What a total turnaround of opinion within a short span of time. A revamp of the international financial arrangements is thus called for. We must accept the fact that the international economic and financial system is seriously flawed because it favours the richer countries. We cannot expect them to change the ground-rules when they are benefiting from it the most.

Most economists agree that "growth is complex and country-specific, and that so many things go into its equation. It's not a simple problem with a simple recipe that can be used for all countries," says Peter Nolan, Professor of Chinese Management at Cambridge University.

According to vice-president and chief economist of the World Bank Joseph E. Stiglitz in the *Asiaweek* of March 27, 1998, "High interest rates and austerity programmes urged by the IMF worsen unemployment. High interest rates and excessively restrictive fiscal policy can have negative effects on domestic demand. ... Excessive currency depreciations, like high interest rates, can also undermine corporations and financial institutions but our econometric studies tend to support the view that high interest rates have a more deleterious effect on financial systems than do devaluations."

James Tobin, Sterling Professor Emeritus at Yale University, who was awarded the Nobel Prize for Economics in 1981 for his work on monetary theory and exchange-rate policies, advocates the lowering of interest rates as a necessary means for economic revival in Asia: "Macroeconomic austerity is not a favourable climate in which to begin long-term structural reforms. In East Asia, the urgent priority is to arrest the plunge in economic activity and start vigorous recovery to restore rates of employment and GDP growth. ... The IMF should support sensible recovery programmes by promising assistance to central banks in sustaining interest reductions to levels consistent with macroeconomic recovery."

Tobin, as you may be aware, proposed that a small fee or transaction tax (known as the "Tobin tax") be charged on all cross-border transactions so as to penalise speculative short-term capital flows. Such a tax is able to discourage short-term currency speculation based on thin margins and yet not impose a heavy burden on long-term investors. According to Christopher Lingle in *The Rise & Decline of the Asian Century: False Starts on the Path to the Global Millennium* (1998), "In essence, the tax would encourage trading that would reflect the needs of the economy and long-run fundamentals, rather than pure market sentiment that is supposedly less committed. ... Tobin's proposal should be viewed as different from those who base their support upon a Marxian-inspired hostility to 'non-productive' activities. From their viewpoint, the justness of taxing foreign-currency deposits is based upon the fact that international capital movements involving portfolio assets like bonds or currencies do not add to national wealth as does direct investment in plant or equipment. Most economists have rejected this logic when they abandoned the allure of mercantilism."

Jeffrey D. Sachs, director of the Harvard Institute for International Development (HIID) and Galen L. Stone Professor of International Trade at Harvard University, and Steven Radelet, an associate at HIID and economics lecturer at Harvard University, have this to say: "After one year, the combination of sustained high interest rates and illiquidity has, in fact, led to severe economic contraction and a vast overhang of bad debt throughout Asia ... The mixture of high interest rates and, rising non-performing loans and IMF pressures for rapid banking recapitalisation has left the entire banking sectors of South Korea, Thailand and Indonesia effectively moribund.

"Under these circumstances, continued high interest rates and the gradual workout of foreign and domestic debts will not solve the problem ... The key is to reduce interest rates and expand credit. Yes, this would probably entail some further depreciation in the region's currencies, at least in the short run. But that would be a relatively small price to pay for restarting economic activity.

"In any event, the impact on exchange rates is likely to be fairly small. Over time, as economic activity picks up and foreign leaders re-enter the markets, exchange rates will again appreciate in real terms. ... There is simply no reason to persist with punishingly high interest rates."

It is hence regrettable that Stanley Fischer, the First Deputy Managing Director of the International Monetary Fund, still insists that the IMF was right on high interest rates and immediate restructuring. For all the chaos and social instability the IMF has caused in the South Korea, Thailand and worst of all Indonesia, Fischer arrogantly dismisses contrary expert views as "an illusion to imagine that there is some painless way of and stability". Surely the IMF could have been less drastic and painful. The same measures could have been gradually introduced with much more compassion and respect for human rights, like eradicating poverty and providing social stability.

If as he claims, "the real issue is how rapidly the underlying structural problems in the financial and corporate sectors are dealt with," how come the IMF did not insist on reforms much earlier? The fact is that their monitoring system was poor and their knowledge of these Asian economies are weak. The IMF is thus guilty of moral hazard and incompetence.

What is even more pathetic about Fischer's essay is that he did not mention the havoc created by unregulated short-term capital flows or "hot money" (where speculators move investments in and out of emerging markets in search of quick profits), which the IMF is studying at a snail's pace.

In the interests of promoting strong and stable economic growth not only in Asia, but all over the world, the outdated IMF has to be reformed to become more relevant to the 21st century. Let us hope some rich and powerful countries will rise to the challenge of leadership.

Bank Negara Malaysia's New Stance in July 1998

Bank Negara Malaysia's latest stance in easing the tight monetary policy pursued earlier with a new framework of liquidity measurement reflects a realistic approach towards reflating the economy. Such an approach will allow for more capital inflows in the monetary system and interest rates can be maintained at more reasonable levels.

Under the new framework announced on July 31, 1998, Bank Negara Malaysia will reduce the three-month intervention rates by 50 basis points to 10.5 per cent. This will most likely reduce the current base lending rate (BLR) at an average of 12.08 per cent by 0.55 per cent to 11.43 per cent. Furthermore, banking institutions are also required to make projections on the maturity profile of their assets to enable the banking institutions to forecast their future liquidity surplus and shortfalls.

The present liquidity framework requires banks to hold a specific amount of liquid assets, amounting to a minimum of 17 per cent of their deposits for commercial banks and 10 per cent for finance companies and merchant banks, and 12.5 per cent, if they issue negotiable instruments of deposits.

However, the reduction of intervention rates would cause an influx of funds in the monetary system, thus raising the possibility of inflationary pressures. Hence, I propose careful monitoring and balancing to avoid excessive inflationary pressures. We have to beware of the impact of inflation because there could be some pressure on inflation as prices will go up when there is an influx of funds.

Overall, the new framework would help ease the tight liquidity in the monetary system and spur the economy to extricate itself from the clutches of recessionary pressures.

Whether the central bank should ease the tight monetary policy further will depend on the situation as it unfolds before making further adjustments. We must fine-tune as we go along and as the economic climate locally and overseas changes.

On the impact of the liquidity relaxation on the ringgit, the Malaysian currency, which is already at a very low level, should be able to hold its own despite the relaxation of interest rates.

The relaxation should not be perceived by foreign investors as inconsistent. We should do what is good for us. Such a move may be described as a Malaysianomic approach, where Malaysians have to do what they want to do in the Malaysian way and in Malaysia's own national interest.

The IMF's lack of transparency and inconsistency in disbursing funds rapidly leaves much to be desired. The way the IMF dealt with the Mexican crisis and its approval of Russia's appeal for US$17 billion (though prodded by Washington) was quick. On the other hand, disbursement of funds to countries in the Asian region, particularly Indonesia, had been stonewalled by the IMF's insistence on imposing and implementing rigid conditions. Of course, while conditions were essential, the IMF must also take into account the plight of the poor in the afflicted countries concerned. The crisis in Asia warrants serious consideration and would require immediate assistance to stimulate the domestic economy and to give confidence to the affected country and the region as a whole. Since there was already a firm commitment by the IMF to assist Indonesia, then the IMF should have made sure the aid is disbursed according to schedule quickly.

The IMF has a critical role to play in overcoming the Asian crisis and some of its recommendations to deal with the Asian crisis are reasonable. But the IMF must learn to appreciate the complexities and peculiarities of each country. Needless to say, countries must undertake to initiate necessary changes and reforms but once the parameters are agreed upon, then disbursement of funds must be fast. The IMF must learn to trust the governments they are dealing with, and not use its power to enforce its own hidden agendas!

Foreign Investment

Relaxation of investment guidelines, which will attract the inflow of long-term funds into the economy, will help to revive the economy faster. The infusion of foreign capital into the economy will go a long way in not only stimulating the domestic economy, but also easing pressure on the demand for domestic funds. To achieve this, the government must exercise greater political will in wanting greater foreign participation in the economy.

The government appears to be reluctant in opening the doors to greater foreign participation for fear of losing its sovereignty or control of ownership. Allowing greater foreign equity ownership and long-term funds may be better alternative to foreign loans which will add to the debt burden of the economy.

While there is very little that the government could do about inflation, as the current inflationary climate in the country is mainly imported inflation due to the declining value of the ringgit against the major currencies. As for the prevailing interest rates in the economy, there is no need to tighten monetary policy further as the higher interest rates in neighbouring countries had not led to massive inflow of funds there. Foreigners were looking at the region as a whole and it is more important to attract long-term investors who will make more meaningful contribution to the economy as opposed to those seeking short-term speculative investment. Short-term speculative funds move in swiftly to take advantage of a bad situation and will move out as quickly too when the situation sours. These short-term funds should be discouraged as they are disruptive.

Services

We must also put more emphasis on the services sector. Malaysia's ticket to ride through the economic downturn lies in developing its services sector to the fullest potential like it did with the industrial sector in the mid-1980s.

Continued deregulation and liberalising of the Malaysian economy must continue if we are to become the regional business and finance centre, as long as it does not undermine our internal monetary policies. But that's why we have the international offshore financial centre in Labuan!

Over the last 10-15 years, the services sector has emerged as the more dynamic sector worldwide, but in Malaysia, its growth rate has remained stunted.

MIT Professor of Economics Paul Krugman, one of the severest critics of the IMF, agrees that Dr Mahathir Mohamad did have a point when he blamed capital market players for the financial crisis, "One of the tragedies of this crisis was that some valid criticisms that a number of people had made were lost because they were wrapped in a lot of irrelevant rhetoric."

Krugman said that IMF reforms had failed and has called for foreign currency controls to put Asian countries back on track. "There has been a lot of repayment but the foreign debt is still a major drag. The point is that you want now to follow a conventional stimulus package. You want Asian economies to respond to their recessions, as if they were the US."

Conclusion

The NEAC has to be congratulated on a sound recovery plan. However, we must overcome the omissions and some concerns as to the expedition in the effective implementation of the recovery plan. By resisting the destructive prescriptions of the IMF and adopting our own brand of "Malaysianomics" to get out of this recession, I believe the National Economic Recovery Plan (NERP) will work, especially if the external environment improves fast. But to really succeed, we need the strong and steady support of all Malaysians and especially a revamped civil service, to recover fully and as soon as possible.

Malaysia must not dwell too much over an immediate economic recovery and instead, should try to stop further decline in the economy by urgently implementing the National Economic Recovery Plan. The NERP has a whole range of recommendations based on in-depth consultation with practically every significant sector of the Malaysian economy. Therefore, it has a wealth of knowledge, ideas and recommendations which the government should adopt and implement urgently.

Chapter 4

HEALING THE WOUNDED TIGER THROUGH SHOCK THERAPY

WHEN the National Economic Recovery Plan (NERP) was first publicised in July 1998, the public felt heartened. They felt that, since there was a comprehensive and substantive plan to combat recession and promote economic recovery, we would be out of the woods soon. The only major concern was the national will and capacity to implement the recovery plan with a sense of urgency. Unfortunately, the problem lies with the velocity of change. Though we have the policies, the speed at which policies are being implemented leaves much to be desired. But time is of essence. *These are unusual times, and such times call for unusual speed and urgency in the formulation and implementation of policies to survive the slump.* In times of boom and rapid economic growth, a little delay in the implementation of policies may not cause problems, but when we are in a recession, like what we are experiencing now, we need to arrest the slide as quickly as possible, before things take a turn for the worse.

That concern has now been reduced by the determination of Dr Mahathir Mohamad to fight recession through the introduction of "shocking measures", such as capital and currency controls and tighter regulations on the stock exchange, further boosted by the early and effective implementation of the National Economic Recovery Plan (NERP).

The business sentiment is now therefore more upbeat and encouraging as a result of the implementation of the NERP, Malaysia's road map to economic and financial recovery.

Capital and currency Controls

The imposition of currency controls and the fixing of the Malaysian currency at RM3.80 to the US dollar are certainly departures from the norm—shocking measures to curb currency manipulation. Dr Mahathir was right in stating earlier that the foreign money market would be shocked. This is because Malaysia has always pursued a liberal and free foreign-exchange system. According to the *Far Eastern Economic Review* of September 17, 1998, "For those who posit that the forces of history are sailing inexorably towards liberal democracy and free-market economics", Malaysia "provided a reality check" by "imposing exchange controls that mark a retreat from the global economy". Of course, such a shocking and drastic move will have its fair share of detractors.

The international money market which is now dominated by currency speculators and manipulators will most probably react unfavourably to our exchange controls for some time, mainly because their own interests will be adversely affected. To what extent they will react, only time will tell.

However, exchange controls are not meant to affect long-term investments, but only speculative short-term capital or "hot money" and stockmarket manipulation. Although more controls and regulations are not really welcomed, under normal circumstances, these controls could be acceptable under the current abnormal circumstances, especially if they are temporary.

It appears we have not much choice in the short term but to introduce and implement shock measures to defend ourselves against the further onslaught of currency manipulators. And, hopefully, with the tighter exchange controls, capital outflows will decline, the balance of payments will improve, and foreign-exchange reserves will rise. Liquidity would then increase in the banking system and interest rates would reduce and thus stimulate more economic activity. All this would hasten economic recovery.

But in the end, only the wider market forces will show how effective or successful these shock measures will be, not only in the short term but later on. Otherwise, we will have to start reviewing the exchange controls in our own national interests. In the meantime, we are taking preemptive measures against any further collapse of other currencies, including the Chinese renminbi.

Multi-Pronged Counter Attack via Malaysianomics
While these shock measures work themselves out, we have to continue on a broader front with other policy measures, to build our longer-term economic fundamentals to fight recession as follows:

First, the most encouraging sign in the gloomy economic environment is the good prospects in the performance of the balance of payments. It will be recalled that the balance of payments was one of the weakest fundamentals when the currency attacks took place in July 1997.

However, it is heartening that for the first six months of 1998, the trade surplus had risen to RM22.1 billion, as compared to only RM2.8 billion for the same period in 1997. This is an impressive increase. There has been some positive response to Dr Mahathir's call to reduce non-essential imports. The drive to expand our exports has been encouraging. The depreciated ringgit that favours exports and raises our export receipts in ringgit have also increased the prospects for our balance of payments to perform even better for the rest of 1998, though it is unlikely that exports alone will be able to pull us out of recession. Exports, of course, will help the economy, but not to a large extent. Recovery will most probably be led by domestic consumption, rather than exports.

The present foreign reserves that are worth four months of our retained imports will rise to much higher levels and will discourage currency manipulators and speculators who could only pay the price for their adventurism and recklessness in currency trade.

The second prong of our attack on recession would be to manage inflation more effectively. For this we have to pursue with our practice of *Malaysianomics*. We will have to be very careful that the hard-won improvements in the balance of payments and the gradual increase in liquidity is channelled scrupulously to really productive projects with high returns. These projects must be selected based on their contribution or ability to save or promote our foreign exchange. We must exercise stronger discipline here to raise our productivity.

Third, banks would have to be more rigorously restructured by Bank Negara Malaysia with the full, professional and political backing of the government.

If there are so-called corrupt cronies, they should be denied access to our hard-earned foreign exchange and liquidity. This is where more transparency and professional management will help tremendously.

Banks that do not meet the more professional or stringent criteria that should be based on world standards should have their licences revoked. After all, these financial institutions are protected in that their licences are limited and not easily available to anyone. These banks actually enjoy monopolistic privileges!

Why should the public therefore pay the price of poor management by these financial institutions, which can only survive with the deposits they amass from the public. *If most of these financial institutions had been more professional and prudent, we would have been better prepared to resist the attacks of unscrupulous currency manipulators.*

Needless to say, Bank Negara Malaysia's supervisory role will have to be further strengthened and its professional integrity protected by a stronger political will.

Foreign Fears

Fourth, having burnt their fingers when the Asian economies collapsed, many foreign investors are now wary of returning to invest due to a lack of confidence in the region. They realise that they were superficial in their assessment of some Asian investments. They know that they were also morally and ethically irresponsible about many of their business decisions in Asia. Thus many of them still do not feel confident about investing in Asia, where they now believe business values and ethics are quite different from their own Western standards. They themselves have made bad judgements and ignored moral hazards.

Thus these foreign investors want to wait till the economic situation stabilises further and when the financial institutions strengthen. They will want to see much more transparency in the conduct of government and business activity before they return to Asia. They also want to wait, to "gobble" up our cheap assets as and when they are cheaper, under the guise of globalisation!

More Shocking Measures

While we wait for more of the NERP measures to be implemented, we should be prepared for more shocking measures to overcome our economic problems. *But what could some of these shocking measures be?*

First, these measures could come from the NERP and they would be shocking only because, unlike previously, they will now be implemented more fully and urgently without political qualms.

Second, some will be shocked if their own vested interests suffer. For instance, the owners of banks and financial institutions who have resisted merging for a long time would be shocked if they are compelled to merge or else their licences will be withdrawn!

Third, imports could be curtailed by more incentives and disincentives so long as they do not encroach on WTO rules.

Fourth, Petronas and the EPF could be required to invest much more in government securities so as to channel more funds to Danaharta and Danamodal. They could also be urged to buy more *Bumiputera* shares as well as more of the blue-chip shares that are now going for a song. This will also help increase the *Bumiputera* share in the corporate sector of the economy. The present preoccupation with *Bumiputera* quotas will then decline and Malaysia could become more globally competitive.

Fifth, the NDP itself could be relaxed further to attract more foreign direct investment without adversely affecting the *Bumiputera* ownership stake of at least 30 per cent in most sectors of the economy. After all, foreign direct investment will continue to remain the key to industrial development in the future. We must continue encouraging new investments in new areas in line with Malaysia's available resources and comparative advantage. The key is to attract long-term investment flows in the areas of high value-added and new technology.

Despite the regional turmoil, Malaysia has made much efforts to provide a smooth passage for FDI, though the onus is now on the genuine, long-haul foreign investors to take advantage of Malaysia's incentives and comparative advantage. Genuine foreign investors should explore new technologies, higher value-added and allow new skill formation amongst Malaysians in the areas of design, research and development and services. FDI assumes an especially heightened role not only to make up for the shortfall in domestic capital formation but more so as a source of new industries and advanced skilled formation amongst the Malaysian workforce.

Sixth, the Industrial Coordination Act 1975 could be relaxed to allow a much higher ceiling than the present restrictive RM2.5

million in capital ownership. This way the large Malaysian Chinese business sector could contribute even more to economic revival.

Seventh, the financial system could be further liberalised by allowing a few selected banks, insurance companies and stockbroking firms to become more foreign owned, even above 50 per cent. This will push our local financial institutions to become even more competitive on a global basis.

Eighth, the land laws could be reformed to enable more state land to be made available for commercial and low-cost housing. This measure would increase food supplies and housing and reduce inflation for especially the poor and low income groups. We sometimes give too much priority to the corporates and much less to the needs of the people and those of the lower-income groups! This measure would be most welcomed by the people.

Ninth, more efficiency could be introduced into the whole economic system at all levels, to enable Malaysia to be much more competitive in the world of rapid globalisation. Thus privatised projects should be made more competitive and shared out more evenly amongst more businessmen on a more balanced basis. A more open and transparent system of awarding privatisation contracts would dismiss lingering doubts and criticisms of cronyism.

Tenth, the IMF itself can be shocked by much more pressure from many more countries to strengthen the international financial architecture. The IMF itself will be shocked with the rising tide of criticism against it and its operations all over the world!

Bretton Woods

Do we need to come up with a new Bretton Woods system? Malaysia could take a stronger leadership role by establishing an international financial reforms centre to complement the initiatives of other industrial and developing countries on what approach to take to create a new Bretton Woods system. The new monetary system would have to be more equitable and relevant to a new world economic order that will not continue to be dominated by the powerful hegemonic forces in the West. (The IMF and World Bank were established as a result of the Bretton Woods agreement, the post-World War II international financial order designed at the landmark 1944 conference in Bretton Woods, New Hampshire.)

We have a leading independent thinker in Lyndon LaRouche in the United States who has courageously called for a new Bretton Woods agreement for a long time. However, he has been sidestepped by the oligarchists who want to serve their own interests.

British Prime Minister Tony Blair has called for the creation of a new Bretton Woods for the new millennium when he spoke at the NYSE on September 21, 1998: "We have to design a new and improved financial architecture for a new age." The role and functions of Bretton Woods institutions such as the IMF and World Bank must be reviewed to keep with changing times because they are no longer capable of handling the new trends in the world economy.

Dr Mahathir has openly criticised the IMF and the hedge-fund operators, and it is hoped that other world leaders will follow suit in jolting the world into reforming the Bretton Woods system and the international financial architecture.

Conclusion

The NERP proposals will have to be implemented expeditiously and further measures introduced even if they shock orthodoxy and some vested interests. In the end, we have to look after Malaysia's own self-interests, survival and progress. Malaysia has about the strongest government in the world with a two-thirds majority.

Malaysians will therefore steadfastly support the government in all its bold initiatives to lift us out of the recession towards economic recovery as long as the government is able to pull us out of this imbroglio, regardless of the shocks involved. And despite recent political setbacks, more specifically the ramifications arising from the removal of Dato' Seri Anwar Ibrahim as deputy prime minister and minister of finance over allegations of misconduct, we will have to be more united at all levels to ensure socio-political stability and to move more purposefully towards economic revival.

The importance of socio-political stability must never be underestimated because civil disruption can lead to chaos and is likely to slow down the return of domestic and foreign investors and economic recovery. We have, in the past, made impressive progress due to social and political stability, and we shall continue to do the same.

Chapter 5

WHERE DO
WE GO FROM
HERE, THEN?

PUBLIC confidence in the quick recovery of the Malaysian economy is on the slide again. About a month ago in July 1998, when the National Economic Recovery Plan was unveiled to much fanfare, the public felt heartened. Since there was a comprehensive and substantive plan to combat recession and promote economic recovery, we felt we would be out of the woods soon. The only concern was whether there is the national will and capacity to implement the recovery plan and deliver the goods.

Today, that concern has turned to anxiety as people wonder why we are still in the long, dark tunnel, and not a glimmer of light at the end of it!

Why is there so very little progress? The main reasons for the slow economic recovery are as follows:

On the external front, the regional contagion continues unabated. South Korea and Indonesia may have hit rock bottom, but their ascent is painfully slow. Indonesia is in the grips of economic, political and social disintegration and will most probably slide even further down the slippery slope.

Japan has a new prime minister in Keizo Obuchi. However, so far he is only so so! He has not shown that he will move as fast as he should to reflate the sluggish Japanese economy. With a shrinking economy, a struggling currency, a slumping stockmarket and seething parliamentary opposition to his reform package, Obuchi has much on his shoulders. The profundity of Japan's economic plight became more apparent as new figures showed the economy contracting again in April-June 1998. It marked the first time since World War II that the nation has experienced a decline over three successive quarters. The latest plunge amounted to a 3.3 per cent shrinkage of the economy on an annualised basis.

China has been thanked at the recent Asean Foreign Minister's meeting in Manila for sparing Asia by not devaluing the renminbi. It can now feel it has done its fair share and that it can now devalue to protect its own interests, especially since Japan, Europe and the United States have been found lacking in their will to do anything significant. *Though how long China can maintain its currency remains to be seen, considering that unemployment is the single biggest problem facing the country today.*

The United States preaches to everyone as to what to do, but it does not do much itself to help Asia. It does not want to bail out the IMF to further aid countries that have to depend on IMF funding despite its conditionalities. Neither does the United States want to do much to reform the international financial architecture nor regulate the movement of destructive hedge-fund operators.

"Gobble-isation"

Globalisation is good, but rapid globalisation, particularly when we are weak, will lead to *"gobble-isation"* by the powerful industrial countries. So the fact of the matter is that this so-called globalisation is really *"gobble-isation"*, with the rich countries all ready to gobble up the assets of the poorer countries, without care or concern for their welfare. It's each country for itself and globalisation for the rich.

The claim by Kassim Ahmad in his article "Present Western leadership has created new world disorder" in the *New Straits Times* of August 1, 1998, and that the "international financial oligarchy" is set to dominate mankind, is worth exploring further. If there is even some truth in this thesis, it is highly dangerous. International think-tanks that are professional and neutral and particularly think-tanks in Asia should investigate the validity of this claim. If it is found to be true, then we should join like-minded people from all over the world to campaign against and eradicate this vicious movement of the "financier oligarchy" or what is now known as the *US Treasury/IMF-Wall Street Complex*, as commented upon by Dato' A. Kadir Jasin in his *New Sunday Times* column, "Other Thots". We need greater international transparency to expose this movement that will suppress the rights of the less fortunate all over the world, most of whom are found in the developing world! This, after all, is the real world!

Domestic Concerns

However, there is not much use berating the situation because it is like banging our heads against the wall. Perhaps some day the walls will crack under their own weight of "creative destruction" due to excessive capitalistic greed. *But, till then, what do the poor countries do?* (Economist Joseph Schumpeter described the aftermath of booms as "creative destruction".)

We need to strengthen our own economic fundamentals. For this we have to avoid the questionable policies and actions that cause uncertainty. What are some of these concerns that may weaken confidence.

First, we must be careful to give the right signals. The recent re-laxation of credit facilities for car purchases could be regarded as the wrong priority at the wrong time. Car purchases are not our priority. They raise consumption, which need not be considered as a wise choice for the majority of consumers with low and middle incomes. Instead more and easier credit should be made available to farmers, the SMIs and house buyers for investment and more durable consumer goods.

Second, while it may be right to believe that we should not be too trusting of the West, we could now perhaps criticise more quietly and less often. After all, it is difficult for anyone to fully trust those who have colonised and exploited us for so long in the past. While we can forgive, it will be naive of us to forget so easily, less we get exploited under new guises.

However, not all Westerners are foreign devils. We have some very sympathetic and empathetic rich industrial countries and individuals in the North who are and can be our friends. We will increasingly need to differentiate countries and individuals in the North as friends and foes. Even then we will need to be careful since foes become friends and friends become foes over time. History has taught us that.

We also have to differentiate more between governments and their peoples. Some government leaders and officials and representatives can be arrogant, condescending and callous. But that is not necessarily true of all their nationals who may themselves resent their leaders and their brazen bullying tactics at home and abroad, People everywhere do not want oligarchists. We have to link up with all those who are like-minded and share common ideals of a more just world.

Malaysia-Singapore relations

Third, ties between Malaysian and Singapore are especially testy these days and will not contribute to efforts at cooperation and goodwill. Foreign investors will be further confused if they find two neighbours who were once one nation having so much trouble.

Regardless of the sovereign rights and legalities of the case regarding the transfer of the Customs, Immigration and Quarantine (CIQ) facili-

ties from Tanjong Pagar to Woodlands, could not the Singapore authorities have handled the issues with more diplomacy and finesse?

All Malaysia asked for on July 28, 1998 was to be given office space inside the new Woodlands railway checkpoint. *Was that too much to ask of a friendly neighbouring country, which was once part of Malaysia?* No, but Singapore had to insist on giving our CIQ space outside—on the platform station. I wonder how Singapore would have reacted if Malaysia had treated Singapore in the same unfriendly manner!

The moral of the story is simple: if you want to be rough with another country, make sure that country is far away—and not your immediate neighbour. How is that for reality, pragmatism and wisdom for the long-term interests of both countries.

With both countries so dependent on each other for trade, investment and even basic needs like drinking water for Singapore, surely the only solution is to consult as members of one big family instead of quarrelling openly as strangers. *What will the neighbours think and say? What will our own people say?* All this does not augur well in strengthening confidence during this time of political and economic uncertainty. I am confident, however, that good sense will prevail for the mutual benefit of both countries.

Ports

Fourth, another concern is the question of urging and even forcing our traders to use our own ports. This could be a useful exercise, especially when we need to step up our foreign-exchange earnings at this time of the crisis. But it would be more prudent in the medium to long term if Malaysian ports can become more efficient and competitive. I do not think that any exporter worth his salt would want to trade through Singapore if it is cheaper and more convenient and efficient to do so through Port Klang.

However, if there is some collusion or conspiracy on the part of some traders, then it would be appropriate for Malaysia to take some drastic action. But we have to find out the real situation before we take radical action to make it mandatory for our exporters and importers to use only our ports. Otherwise, we may be sending the wrong signals again to the business world. We may also run foul of the WTO. However, the Minister of Transport, Dato' Seri Dr Ling Liong Sik, is working hard to improve the situation and I believe he will solve some of these problems.

SMIs

Fifth, many would share former Minister of Finance Dato' Seri Anwar Ibrahim's dissatisfaction and concern that just RM253 million has been disbursed to only 187 loan applicants out of an allocation of RM1,500 million, so far.

The problem is mainly with the twenty large financial institutions which have been tardy in their analysis and disbursement of loans for SMIs. How can they treat those small businessmen whose needs are greatest with such indifference and lack of priority and commitment.

But merely reprimanding the slack financial institutions is not satisfactory. They must be pulled up and penalised. *How can huge banks be giving out so few loans?* The government must also be seen to be fair to SMIs by forcing the banks to do their duty diligently or punish them for their lack of empathy and cooperation. (This idea has now been accepted as banks are required to step up lending to 8 per cent per annum and to increase their profit margins to 2.5 per cent above the BLR.)

Otherwise, credibility will suffer, particularly since the Special Purpose Vehicle, Danamodal, is meant to clean up the balance sheets of adversely affected banks and then recapitalise them.

Then again it is disappointing that despite the government's long-drawn urging, the banks and finance companies are still not merging. In South Korea, Thailand and Indonesia, and even in Japan, financial institutions are merging much faster. This is necessary to strengthen the banking system and to enable our financial institutions to compete with the foreign financial giants that we will have to compete with in the near future. The relentless pressure of the rich countries through the World Trade Organisation to force us to open up to our banks is continuing, and if local banks are weak and small, they will be *gobble-ised* via globalisation.

Even now, the foreign banks in Malaysia are making serious inroads into our financial system because of their enormous backing in funding and in R&D on the latest technology and products. With electronic banking, these foreign banks do not need new branches or new buildings, which could be expensive liabilities instead.

Bank Negara Malaysia could be actively encouraged to speed up the process of consolidation and enhancing efficiency in our financial system. Otherwise, we will face grave financial and funding problems in the near future. It is, however, encouraging that Bank Negara Malaysia is now insisting on a new framework which is modelled along international best practices in the management of our financial system.

I would have thought that a year since the crisis burst upon us, these best practices would have been introduced earlier. However, little has been done. But better a little late than much later or never!

We do not seem to be moving fast enough. This is symptomatic of our problems. We seem to be still slow to react and respond rapidly in areas where there is no threat to social disruption. To the extent that we delay acceptable reforms, we will face domestic and especially foreign criticism and uncertainty as to our national will to manage the current recession effectively and expeditiously.

The government will need to fix specific target dates for bank mergers and enforce them, in order to build greater confidence in our financial system, which provides the fuel to accelerate our economic recovery! Indeed, we need a greater sense of urgency in whatever we do, otherwise we will not go far in our recovery efforts.

Debt Restructuring

It is good that former Minister of Finance Dato' Seri Anwar Ibrahim has announced the formation of a steering committee and various credit committees to restructure the debt of our corporates with loans exceeding RM50 million. This Corporate Debt Restructuring Committee (CDRC) will be able to rescue some of the better corporates that are in trouble as a result of the economic turmoil.

Too many of our corporates were going to the law courts for protection against creditors, especially banks, for demanding repayment of loans. As a result of which, the law courts were getting jammed up. Some corporates could be abusing the protection provided under Section 176(1) of the Companies Act 1965. In the end, the creditors and particularly the financial institutions would suffer. Non-performing loans of the banks, now estimated at around 10 per cent, could deteriorate further. This trend will weaken the financial system further and cause a greater erosion of confidence and eventually capital flight and all its bad consequences.

Conditions

This move by the government to rescue large corporates is most timely, but there must be conditions to ensure the effective restructuring of corporate debt as follows:

First, seeking advice from the Steering and Credit Committee (SCC) should not be on a voluntary basis. If companies cause banks to weaken, the public will suffer. So it should be incumbent upon corporates to refer their debt restructuring to the SCC immediately. There must be some compulsion.

Second, it should also be made conditional for these seriously indebted companies to refer their proposals for debt restructuring to the SCC first before they apply to the Court for protection under the Companies Act 1965.

Third, while RM50 million is an appropriate minimum debt to refer to the SCC, the minimum could be lowered to a lesser amount, even down to RM10 million. There are many companies that are in trouble with smaller debt. The smaller corporates must be subject to similar discipline to restructure their debt, much sooner.

Fourth, it is important that the whole credit settlement exercise is transparent and that preference and priority will not be given to favoured companies. The selection criteria should be applied to all seriously indebted companies, regardless of their connections to strong vested groups.

Finally, the SCC will undoubtedly generate confidence, but it must ensure that the reputable leading institutions with professionally qualified designated managers will be carefully selected, to complete all the five stages of approval of debt restructuring within short and specific time schedules.

Although this corporate credit settlement exercise started early on August 19, 1998, it is just as important to aim for a target date to complete the whole exercise of all the major debt-ridden companies in Malaysia. This is a major structural adjustment which calls for concerted and urgent action.

New Institutions

The setting up of Pengurusan Danaharta Nasional (Danaharta) and Danamodal Nasional (Danamodal) and a Steering and Credit Committee to help ailing banks and finance companies restructure their debts are excellent pre-emptive strategies. Both Danaharta and Danamodal would complement and reinforce each other in safeguarding and strengthening the banking and financial system to accelerate the rate of economic recovery.

The Special Purpose Vehicle established to recapitalise local banks will now be called more meaningfully Danamodal. By recapitalising domestic banking institutions to healthy levels and enhancing their ability to generate new lending, Danamodal will also facilitate the consolidation and rationalisation of the banking sector. Although its initial seed money is only RM1.5 billion, the whole recapitalisation exercise could amount to over RM16 billion if the risk-weighted capital adequacy ratio (CAR) is to be maintained at 9 per cent. (The Bank for International Settlements set the minimum risk-weighted capital adequacy ratio at 8 per cent.)

Danaharta, on the other hand, is a national asset management company established by the government on June 20, 1998 to revitalise the Malaysian financial sector by purchasing or removing the distraction of managing non-performing loans (presently estimated at 10 per cent of their assets) from financial institutions and thus enabling them (the financial institutions) to focus their attention on their core business activity which is to lend to viable borrowers and to maximise the recovery value of the acquired assets and liabilities through specialist skills in managing the NPLs. A re-energised financial sector will enhance confidence and assist in revitalising the Malaysian economy. The funds necessary for such an exercise could amount to as much as RM$15 billion.

The big question is how do we raise all these huge funds?

Since three international rating agencies have downgraded the credibility and strength of Malaysia's financial system, the proposed roadshows to raise foreign funding have been postponed. This is understandable as the timing for issuing new bonds is important if we are to obtain sufficient volumes and good prices for bond sales. But we cannot afford to wait too long because in the meantime, our banks remain undercapitalised as the non-performing loans keep rising and the financial system weakens.

Although the three new financial institutions—Danamodal, Danaharta and the Steering and Credit Committee—to restructure corporate debt need to get into action, it is equally important that they get cracking at a faster pace. If our capacity and expertise to move faster on these innovative measures are limited, then let us hire the best foreigners available, to get on with the job of restructuring our debt-ridden companies, recapitalising weak banks and rehabilitating their high non-performing loans.

Conclusion

Time is of the essence now. The longer we take to get going, the more serious will our problems become, and the more difficult it will be to build confidence and to attract sorely needed foreign invest-ments and funding. In the meantime, let us tap the resources at our disposal, such as from well-endowed domestic institutions like Petronas, the EPF and the Pilgrimage Fund Board (Lembaga Tabung Haji), and start moving at a quicker pace. *There are sufficient re-sources domestically to help the weaker banks and corporates keep their heads above water. We need to stop the rot fast; otherwise, we will slide into deeper recession.*

We must also grapple with the possibility of a global economic recession which could impede our recovery plans, considering that almost half the world economy is already affected by the so-called Asian contagion.

Chapter 6

CAPITAL & CURRENCY CONTROLS: NOT EVERYONE'S CUP OF TEA

THE Malaysian economy is healing with the implementation of new measures to restore dynamism to the economy. Domestic confidence in the economy is rising. Despite the criticism of many Western financial analysts, the capital and currency controls and other NERP policy measures are helping Malaysia to recover.

The ringgit has been fixed at RM3.80 per US dollar and is faring well. The business community is relieved of the previously erratic currency fluctuations. International trade can now be planned and promoted with greater certainty. The Malaysian stockmarket has also become more buoyant. This will have a salutary effect on the performance of the non-performing loans that have been backed by Malaysian stocks and shares.

The tide could well be turning in Malaysia's favour. Even the staid *Financial Times* of London has come out in support of Malaysia's capital and currency controls instituted on September 1, 1998.

The *Financial Times* mentioned three factors that are necessary for the imposition of currency controls in the short term. They are:

the limitation of controls to speculative short-term capital flows (this is exactly what we have done); the controls should be simple (that is also what we have done); and capital controls must be used to assist reforms (here too the condition has been fulfilled by the many reforms that are being implemented through Danaharta, Danamodal and the restructuring of corporate debt).

There are also many other measures to tighten the supervision of the market as introduced by the Securities Commission, the KLSE and Bank Negara Malaysia.

So, it is not exactly a case of imposing capital and currency controls and sitting back and ignoring the need to strengthen and reform our financial institutions. But admittedly we have to undertake more internal economic as well as international financial reforms.

International Reforms

But what are the United States and other rich industrial countries doing to reform the outdated international monetary system? Hitherto, very little, unfortunately. They seem to be dragging their feet. *Why?* Because they think they will not be adversely affected by the economic crisis in Asia. But they could not be more wrong. The United States and some European economies are already being affected by the financial crisis. The so-called Asian contagion could spread to the West and might bring about a worldwide recession if we are not careful. Only then would they be forced to react, but by then, it will most probably be too late, for the world as well!

The United States and Europe have to act more forcefully now to save themselves, even if they do not give a hoot about Asia. The dysfunctional Japanese banking system is creaking under its own weight. At the end of September 1998, the high-flying John Meriwether's Long-Term Capital Management (LTCM) Corp hedge fund suffered massive losses to the tune of US$4 billion and had to be bailed out by the US Federal Reserve Board in excess of US$4 billion. LTCM drew on credit lines from global financial institutions to take positions in derivatives valued at US$100 billion at one point. Many of those bets are turning sour. With the near collapse of LTCM, it looks like Malaysia's complaints about unbridled currency trading have finally proved valid. (Connecticut-based LTCM suffered massive losses after launching a speculative attack on the Russian rouble, resulting in several banks being left with no choice but to supply it with large loans. As a result of this debacle, there is a possibility of many more hedge funds and banks collapsing *en masse*.) The Federal Reserve Board, America's central bank, engineered the rescue because it feared more turmoil in the world's financial system. Coming in the wake of Russia's debt default, the LTCM debacle ought to shock and shake the United States out of its complacency. I believe the West has been caught by surprise that the practice of cronyism is far wider in the United States!

Many Western policymakers consider the outflow of capital from Asia, Russia and Latin America as "a just penalty for flawed policies and corrupt crony capitalism". This view no longer holds water in the light of the collapse and rescue of LTCM. *So, is this bailout some kind of Western crony capitalism? If not, when exactly is a bailout not a bailout? Perhaps it depends on where it occurs?*

According to the *Financial Times*, "The LTCM hedge-fund fiasco has exposed not only inept banking practice from Wall Street via Switzerland to the Italian central bank, but a surprising degree of cronyism in the West; a cronyism less corrupt than in Indonesia or Russia, but with more dangerous consequences, given the scale of the financial risks involved. ... But the rescue of LTCM has revealed relationships that smack of cronyism and potential conflicts of interest. One concerns the involvement of the Federal Reserve in brokering the fund's controversial rescue. 'Why?' asked former Fed chairman Paul Volcker this week, '*should the weight of the federal government be brought to bear to help out a private investor? It's not a bank.*' The only respectable answer is that the Fed believed the collapse of LTCM would have posed a threat to the whole US banking system." Enough said.

Hypocrisy and double standards

The LTCM fiasco is a classic case of hypocrisy and double standards on the part of the financial authorities of the United States and those who criticise Asia for economic and financial mismanagement. They attribute the Asian crisis to crony capitalism. Here you have a case of a huge bailout of a hedge fund to protect private individuals. It was not a case of the rescue being made voluntarily but Alan Greenspan, the chairman of the US Federal Reserve, using his influence with obvious US government backing to rescue this failed enterprise. *If the US authorities are so keen to on free trade and liberalisation, why did they intervene in the markets? And why do they oppose others from intervening in the markets as in Asia. Is it not crony capitalism at its worst?* This episode underlines the urgency for regulations which will minimise the abuses of ultra-liberalisation in the global financial system. There is a need for new rules to pre-empt the gambling phenomenon of hedge funds.

In the meantime, as Dr Mahathir Mohamad explained at a recent meeting of the Malaysian Business Council (MBC), we cannot afford to wait for others to move; we must "insulate" Malaysia from the vagaries of global market forces, more specifically the vicious and volatile currency attacks as a matter of greatest urgency. That is why we have invoked capital and currency controls. With exchange controls, investors need not suffer the rude shock of a collapsing ringgit as a consequence of foreign-currency attacks.

How long will these exchange controls be enforced? It is difficult to put a time frame because we have to take into account many other variables. Though the exchange controls are not permanent, they will remain as long as they are necessary to revive the economy and minimise the impact of speculative short-term capital flows. Of course, we would like remove the exchange controls once the Malaysian economy strengthens. But there is no point lifting the controls if no mechanism is instituted to regulate and control speculators and short-term capital movements in the international financial architecture. Though changes in the global financial architecture is going to take some time, and Malaysia cannot afford to wait that long.

Dr Mohamed Ariff, executive director of the Malaysian Institute of Economic Research (MIER), warns, "We must resist the temptation to keep exchange controls longer than necessary. If exchange controls work in the short term, there may be a temptation to continue with it. If exchange controls do not work, there may be attempts to make them work by tightening the controls. We must guard ourselves against such pitfalls, as the slope is extremely slippery."

Capital and currency controls are aimed at building domestic confidence in the economy. Once domestic confidence in the economy has been restored, foreign investors would return. These new measures are not there to frighten foreign investors. They are there to "insulate" the Malaysian economy from short-term speculators. Sudden movements of large amounts of short-term capital in and out of the economy will affect exchange rates and economic stability. The main objective of the exchange controls is to enable Malaysia to regain monetary independence and "insulate" the Malaysian economy from the prospects of further deterioration in the global economic and financial climate so as to put Malaysia on the path to recovery.

We must understand that the previous measures to revive the economy failed dismally and were adopted on the advice of the IMF, so that foreigners would invest in Malaysia. But somehow these measures failed as foreigners fought shy of investing in Malaysia. And when we started registering a growth of negative 2.8 per cent in the first quarter and negative 6.8 per cent in the second quarter of 1998, it was blatantly clear we needed to lower interest rates to revive business sentiment. However, if interest rates were lowered, then it will result in further depreciation of the ringgit followed by the outflow of the ringgit. And to staunch the outflow of ringgit, the currency, as of October 1, 1998, was made no longer freely tradeable overseas. Any ringgit outside the country would be illegal tender overseas and ringgit movements in and out of the country would be subject to stringent declaration. Besides, the ringgit was pegged at RM3.80 to the US dollar.

There are immediate benefits to capital controls: foreign reserves will go up, the fixed exchange rate will hold at RM3.80 to the US dollar, leading to the easing of interest rates. But we must, of course, be aware that such measures only work in the short term and that the benefits will be shortlived as they would dry up long-term FDI and raise the spectre of a black market in ringgit. Though chances of that happening is unlikely because Malaysia has a strong current-account surplus, a low level of foreign debts and our foreign-exchange reserves are rising. In the meantime, we will have to continue strengthening our financial institutions and assist the SMIs as well as big businesses by restructuring them to overcome their debt problems and becoming more efficient and globally competitive. Capital controls, if well planned and well timed, can work well in the long term and bring about stable exchange rates and overall stability to the economy.

UNCTAD has given Malaysia a vote of confidence by recommending that other developing countries could adopt similar measures as protection or "insulation" from the vicissitudes of the world's financial market instability. According to an UNCTAD official, Yilmaz Akyuz, "For the Malaysian situation, the implementation was out of necessity and not due to its ideology. Although there would be cost to the implementation, it would nevertheless allow for stability so that the country could continue with recovery efforts." Currency control had been a proven technique in dealing with volatile capital flows, and would remain an indispensable part of developing countries' armoury of measures for protection against international financial instability. In a report released in September 1998, UNCTAD says, "Turning a blind eye to the systemic nature of financial instability is neither responsible nor acceptable. Global surveillance and regulation have lagged behind the integration of financial markets—with increasingly costly consequences."

Salomon Smith Barney:
New Financial Advisers

This is where the newly appointed financial experts, US investment bank Salomon Smith Barney (SSB), the securities firm controlled by financial services giant Citigroup Inc, comes in. (Salomon Smith Barney was created from the merger of Salomon Brothers and Smith Barney following the acquisition of Salomon by Travelers Group Inc in 1977.) They could strengthen and reinforce our efforts to rehabilitate and modernise our financial system without having to go to the IMF or even submit to the pressures of foreigners intent on taking over our financial institutions. The appointment of SSB as advisers to the government is thus a strategic move for several reasons.

First, we need a world-class financial consulting firm, especially an American one, to promote Malaysia in the Western-dominated international financial centres. Foreign financial experts somehow listen to their own kind much more readily than they would listen to us, even if we say the same things.

Second, many of our own people will feel more confident that a highly reputed global financial firm is giving us advice and has the capacity to deliver our message abroad. *After all, a prophet is never recognised in his own country.*

Third, even the great philosopher and futurist Alvin Toffler has described IMF policies as "not only stupid and arrogant, it got people killed". So we need the advice of other Western institutions to replace the IMF's questionable advice to Malaysia.

Fourth, Salomon Smith Barney will be able to convince the Western ultra-liberals and the international community that there must be global monetary reform to enable small developing countries like Malaysia to achieve economic growth with social stability. They have to dismiss the views of the foreign media and financial analysts that we have "closed our economy to the global capital market". The West must be persuaded that there are alternate economic paths to achieving socio-economic progress with equity and fair-

103

ness, for rich and poor alike, and not only for the big, rich and powerful countries.

Fifth, we need more funds to recapitalise our banks through Danamodal and to reduce our NPLs through Danaharta. SSB could be the best bet to raise these funds domestically and especially in foreign money markets. Then we will need to borrow less from the US-dominated World Bank and can continue to keep the IMF at bay. But SSB will also have to ensure that we do not borrow too much and at unduly high prices. Otherwise, SSB itself will fail us. There are already some who question SSB in its success in persuading Western money markets to appreciate the need for our exchange controls. Looks like SSB will have to do more.

Exchange controls do not mean a slowdown of direct foreign investment in productive activities. SSB must convince the world that the fixed exchange rate would facilitate the planning of investment budgets and processing of goods for the domestic and international markets and that Malaysia will continue to pursue pro-business policies for those investing here for the long haul. There will also be no restrictions in the repatriation of profits, dividends and capital. The business community, both local and foreign, should welcome these currency controls as costly hedging is no longer necessary. The measures are thus aimed at containing speculation on the ringgit and minimising the impact of short-term capital inflows on the domestic economy.

During a period of economic restructuring, there is bound to be much apprehension amongst foreign investors. The prolonged economic and financial crisis since July 1997 has resulted in a serious contraction in the economies of the region after a decade of rapid economic growth. Malaysia was not spared from this turbulence which had resulted in the contraction in almost all sectors of the economy in the first two quarters 1998 (where real GDP growth shrank by 2.8 per cent and 6.8 per cent respectively).

Against the continued adverse global developments, Malaysia had no other alternative but to take radical measures to put a stop to the basic causes of the economic downturn, that is, manipulative devaluation of the currency and the rapid withdrawal of capital from the share market.

SSB believes that capital controls, a fixed exchange rate and easier monetary policies "should improve [the] government's ability to bring forward the timing of economic recovery". According to the US investment bank, "The measures will help reduce corporate Malaysia's collective balance sheet, which means lower non-performing loans and greater success of corporate debt restructuring." But to make sure all these work, Malaysia must win the faith and confidence of local and foreign investors that its strategy will work and thereby stop capital flight. They must also convince bankers and investors that Malaysia remains a solid sovereign credit risk by reassuring them about the likely impact of capital controls and the government's commitment to banking and corporate restructuring.

Reservations

However, the real economy must also be given priority. The farmers, the fishermen, the estate workers and the small- and medium-scale businessmen from both rural and urban areas must also be looked after. There are reservations about doing too much for big business at the expense of the less fortunate. This is where the government should allocate more budgetary funds to alleviate poverty and unemployment.

Infrastructure projects that are essential for boosting economic development must also be carried on. But there must be more stringent criteria to ensure that only highly productive and foreign-exchange saving or earning projects are provided the necessary funding. Less productive and low-priority projects should be scrupulously scratched out of the long lists of application for funds and bailouts.

The regular NEAC Reports on the progress made by the recovery plan have to be much more substantive, to do justice to the NERP's many sound recommendations. Otherwise, the public might feel that the recovery plan is not moving fast enough to help the real economy, i.e. the people. But whatever we do to restore the economy the people will suffer unless there is international financial reform. But the United States, Europe and Japan or the G7 industrial countries are only still paying lip service so far. They will not care until they are adversely affected by the crisis themselves!

APEC Currency Liberalisation

The recent currency controls could be regarded as a contravention of the aims to liberalise further in anticipation of the Asia-Pacific Economic Cooperation (APEC) Summit on November 17-18, 1998 in Kuala Lumpur. John Wolf, the US Ambassador to APEC and former Ambassador to Malaysia, has already stated that exchange controls will erode global monetary stability. *How rhetorical and ironical can we get?* Their financial institutions attack us and that's nothing!

In fact, Malaysia's exchange controls were adopted in order to promote monetary stability in Malaysia by "insulating" our economy against currency manipulators who have caused major instability in the monetary and the real economies in many Asian countries. If exchange controls have a constraining effect on international trade, so be it. If the currency manipulators and rich countries suffer from the deprivation of opportunities to profit at our experience, it can't be helped. After all they have done hardly anything to prevent this mess, although they could have done a great deal to help through the IMF and through international monetary reforms.

We were therefore very careful about our stance at the 6th APEC Summit in Kuala Lumpur on November 17-18, 1998. This is not the time to liberalise and globalise when these same liberal policies actually precipitated the currency and economic crisis in Thailand first and then deepened and spread to many Asian countries.

Let us urge the United States and other major currency players at APEC to reform the international monetary system first before developing countries take additional steps to liberalise over and above what we have already committed to do.

We must ensure that we do not succumb to undue pressure to serve the interests of the few rich and powerful countries in APEC, the Caucasian countries led by the United States, and Japan, which sometimes does not seem to realise where it belongs or where its long-term interests lie!

International Monetary Reform and Changing Tides

When Dr Mahathir Mohamad urged the IMF to initiate international monetary reform and regulate hedge funds at the IMF-World Bank Meeting in Hong Kong in September 1997, he was described by currency speculator George Soros as "a menace" and a danger to Malaysia, after singling out Soros, whose trading practices Dr Mahathir labelled as "immoral". No one supported Dr Mahathir then. Many experts even derided the idea at that time, dismissing his urging as an embattled leader's weak attempt to blame speculators for Malaysia's economic woes.

When Malaysia criticised the work of the IMF in South Korea, Thailand and Indonesia, the IMF stoutly defended itself as right and reasonable.

But it looks like the tides have changed now and Malaysia is becoming less of a "heretic" for its capital controls. Dr Mahathir has proved to be right in his insight and instincts. A host of eminent economists are now saying there must be monetary reforms and that short-term capital flows must be subject to some form of supervision and regulation.

Paul Krugman agrees that currency controls are acceptable in the short term because such measures "... must serve as an aid to reform, not an alternative. The breathing room given by controls should be used to accelerate, not slow, the pace of financial cleanup." Though temporary currency controls are part of the solution for Asia, Krugman warns that the imposition of currency controls is a risky step, where success in not guaranteed. In an open letter to Dr Mahathir, he warns, "... It is, as many people have pointed out, a stopgap measure. There is no shame in that: some gaps desperately need to be stopped. For the new policy to succeed, however, the freedom of action achieved by your willingness to defy orthodoxy must be well used." However, Krugman warns that "... this policy departure should be purely and simply to buy space for economic growth. It should not be used in an attempt to prove points about the soundness of the pre-crisis economy, or about the wickedness of hedge funds, or anything else. If Malaysia truly does succeed in achieving a recovery, that will be lesson enough for the rest of us."

Of course, Malaysia must make sure it makes good use of this temporary "breathing room". Otherwise, there is a dangerous tendency that capital controls may bring about a sense of complacency and result in a delay in needed reforms.

Nobel Prize-winning economist Dr Milton Friedman has even suggested that the IMF and the World Bank should be shut down and "to disappear" as they have outlived their role and usefulness. He claimed they had done more harm than good to the developing economies. "Unfortunately, both the IMF and the World Bank have tended to strengthen government's projects work against private business. So the best thing they could do is to disappear."

The IMF itself has now admitted its mistakes in dealing with the Asian financial crisis. Even George Soros, once averse to financial trading curbs, now agrees that there is a need for greater surveillance and regulation of capital flows, and has called for restraint on capital movement "to protect countries from the onslaught of the wrecking ball". Soros admits that "a totally free flow of capital is not advisable" and can be destructive. "Instead of acting like a pendulum, financial markets acted more like a wrecking ball, knocking over one economy after another."

So, Dr Mahathir's bold initiative is finding more and more support. Even President Clinton has now called for a meeting of world finance ministers and central bank governors to consider steps to shore up the global financial system within 30 days while addressing the Council of Foreign Relations in New York on September 14, 1998. Hopefully, President Clinton's calls for monetary reforms will actually lead to concrete action, otherwise his calls could end up as rhetoric and red herrings to detract attention from his alleged "inappropriate relationship" with former White House intern Monica Lewinsky.

But on October 1, 1998, the IMF's Chief Economist Michael Mussa changed the traditional stand and called for the lowering of interest rates to restore damaged business and investor confidence. What an about-turn of policy considering the havoc the IMF has caused!

Concerns Over Currency Controls

In Malaysia, while the currency controls were felt to be right and proper in the short term, there were concerns over their continuation in the longer term.

The most significant disadvantage is psychological. Malaysia was one of the few developing countries that had been relatively free of exchange controls. It, therefore, came as a shock to the international markets that even Malaysia has taken what is regarded by the market as a retrograde step.

Given the often obsessive bias of those fanatically committed to the free market, they immediately imagined that we are not just "insulating" ourselves from currency manipulators but "isolating" ourselves from the Western concepts of free trade, globalisation and liberalisation.

Thus, although FDI will not be subject to foreign-exchange controls, there are many long-term investors who now question whether their investment, both existing and potential, will be subject to exchange controls in the future. *They argue that if we can impose exchange controls suddenly on short-term capital flows or "hot money", what assurance is there that Malaysia will not change the rules of the game again and apply controls to the repatriation of dividends and profits and even the capital of genuine foreign direct investors?* This is a concern and challenge we have to face. Some long-term foreign investors have even suggested that they will find it easy to invest in Malaysia, under the new regime of foreign-exchange controls, only if they can get a kind of government guarantee that their investment funds and profits can be repatriated anytime in the future. It is a serious question of confidence!

Short-term foreign investors will invest in the KLSE, only if they can send their funds abroad sooner than one year after investing in the market. Otherwise, they will avoid the KLSE and cause it to remain slow and sluggish.

The challenge for the NEAC is therefore to find ways and means to further refine our foreign-exchange controls as soon as possible. We must further encourage long-term investors and discourage the real short-term currency and share market manipulators. We must show a distinct difference in the treatment of the manipulators and the genuine investors. The transaction tax on "hot money" (like those Chile has employed) is one way of doing so, but there are many international experiences and examples (the Tobin tax, for instance) on how to focus on reducing currency and stock-market manipulation, that we can easily adopt. It is thus imperative that the NEAC address these issues with a greater sense of urgency.

Challenging the Status Quo

However, the biggest challenge to our economy will be the speed with which we can revert back to the *status quo* of freedom from foreign-exchange controls or to adopt very focused controls on disruptive "hot money" only.

While Dr Mahathir is laudable succeeding in gaining more international support for global monetary reform, it will take some time before the rich and powerful industrial countries do much about monetary reform and the IMF.

We may not be able to wait that long. Since our economy is stabilising, our balance of payments is improving and our foreign reserves increasing, after the introduction of exchange controls, we could relax our new exchange controls sooner rather than later.

The risk of delay in reverting to a free exchange regime is that, we may move from reasonable "insulation" to complacency and then some "isolation" from the world of increasing competition. That would be counter productive if not equally disruptive to achieving our longer-terms goals of rapid industrialisation and modernisation under Vision 2020.

We must also be careful to ensure that the respite from currency attacks that we now enjoy will be used to strengthen our financial system. Huge financial resources are now being used and raised domestically and abroad, to save some of our ailing institutions like Sime Bank, Bank Bumiputra, etc. These scarce funds have to be judiciously applied to help the most deserving and high priority enterprises that are worthy of the government's innovative efforts and our sacrifices. After all, more debt means more burdens for us and future generations.

Those companies that are rescued must improve their performance, otherwise it will be like pouring hard-earned money into holes in the ground. Even a renowned international financial house like Salomon Smith Barney will have problems convincing our prospective financiers, investors and foreign friends, if we do not hasten the process of financial reform and restructuring on a professional basis. Therefore, although the exchange controls are bold and timely, we need to move fast to reform or risk wasting the time that we have now gained to pursue policies of rapid economic recovery. In the meantime we have to prepare for the 1999 Budget.

The 1999 Budget

The 1999 Budget will be presented by the Prime Minister and First Minister of Finance Dato' Seri Dr Mahathir Mohamad on October

23, 1998. However, there is little excitement and lesser speculation on what the new Budget plans and proposals will be. This is because we know there can't be many tax goodies!

Hopefully, the Budget will contain measures to further revive and boost the economy by reinforcing the measures already in place to stabilise the economy through the NERP.

Too many important developments on the political and economic fronts and even the very successful 16th Commonwealth Games held in Kuala Lumpur have overshadowed the prospects for the 1999 Budget. Dato' Seri Anwar Ibrahim, the former Deputy Prime Minister and Minister of Finance, had been sacked and the National Economic Recovery Plan was introduced with a wide range of economic and monetary measures to hasten economic recovery.

So there is very little left that has not already been proposed for consideration in the 1999 Budget—the last for this century and this millennium!

Indeed, I believe that the 1999 Budget will practically be a non-Budget. The only issues to be dealt with will be the expenditure allocations and any new taxes.

The expenditure allocations will be somewhat constrained as we do not want a deficit. With the depressed revenue collections from an economy in serious recession, we cannot expect a surplus even on the Budget's current account. We could raise taxes to overcome or reduce a Budget current-account deficit, but this is not the time to reduce too many taxes.

At the most we could have lower income tax rates and some selective reduction of import duties and sales taxes, to alleviate the burden of the corporate sector and the lower income groups. But there are major constraints. We cannot afford to borrow to pay the salaries of civil servants. It would be fiscally imprudent in the longer term.

At the same time the expenditure allocations on the operating budget, meant to maintain and run the government agencies such as agriculture, health, education and security cannot be cut back too much.

Nevertheless, we could have an overall budget deficit, with more allocations made for development expenditures. This will be necessary to expand our infrastructure in transport, water reservoirs, schools, hospitals and housing.

This overall deficit will have to be financed by additional domestic and foreign borrowing. But these are serious limitations as to how much more we can borrow, although our external debt is relatively low. Too much borrowing will rapidly increase our national debt and out future generations have to bear the debt burden.

Danaharta and Danamodal will also have to increase their borrowing to reduce NPLs and to recapitalise weak banks.

The existing bureaucratic constraints to legal business activity and economic growth must also be removed. For instance, there are many outmoded bureaucratic requirements especially in the housing industry and land alienation. There are at present many legal and policy constraints in the Industrial Coordination Act 1975 stifling the SMIs, which provide the backbone to our local industries. These constraints could be removed in the 1999 Budget.

Where there are *Bumiputera* quotas, in housing and SMIs, they can at least be temporary relaxed, to stimulate economic revival. *We can't have the cake and eat it too.* All Malaysians must make an effort to contribute towards economic recovery. Otherwise, our recovery will be slow and long drawn!

Economic Revival

There are already signs that the economy is not declining but slowly picking up. The balance of payments are improving, the reserves are rising and Malaysian capital is flowing in. Car sales and housing starts will pick up further with the recent relaxation of bank credit.

This will also further strengthen the stockmarket. What we need now is to summon our confidence and look forward with a will to succeed.

The present unfortunate political crisis should not be regarded as a setback to businessmen who in the final analysis need political stability and a conducive business-friendly government, to increase investment and prosper. However, we will need more economic reforms in order to build more confidence in our capacity to revive the economy.

It is encouraging that Dr Mahathir has reiterated that the ringgit is now fixed at an exchange rate of RM3.80 to the US dollar and that he will not review the rate until the exchange rates of competing currencies become too wide and affect Malaysia's competitiveness.

It is vital to ensure that the exchange rate for the ringgit is realistically related to the actual market rate. If there is a black market for the ringgit, then the exchange rate must be adjusted from time to time so that trade, investment and business confidence will be enhanced.

The National Economic Recovery Plan (NERP) has many good policy proposals that are still not implemented. There is therefore a rich reservoir of recommendations that could be adopted by the 1999 Budget. We therefore look forward to a meaningful and proactive 1999 Budget.

On the whole, the borrowing by the Budget and the economy as a whole will rise considerably. Thank goodness that Malaysia's foreign debt is still relatively small. However, it is mounting. There is a limit to our borrowing, before it causes strains on the economy. We have to be careful that we do not borrow more than we can bear, otherwise our economic capacity to revive and recover will be impaired and prolonged.

The 1999 Budget must be carefully planned. While we need to help the corporate sector, the banks and particularly the low income

114

groups, we also need to ensure that the 1999 Budget does not generate too much economic strain and instability through too much borrowing. There has to be a cautious approach and prudent balance between promoting economic revival and maintaining financial stability.

The overriding consideration however is to continue to have political and social stability. This has differentiated Malaysia from almost the whole of the developing world.

The dismissal of former Deputy Prime Minister Dato' Seri Dr Anwar Ibrahim is unfortunate and a cause for concern. It has already caused some social unrest. I hope that the current problems will be resolved and that the road to economic recovery will be clear, to move faster towards sustained economic growth and stability.

Monetary System Reforms

The IMF managing director has finally called for a broad reform of the world's international financial system, including the IMF itself. According to IMF managing director Michel Camdessus in a commentary published in *The Washington Post* of September 27, 1998, "The reform of the IMF itself will have to be part of the major overhaul."

Developing countries have always been allowed too little say in determining the IMF's approach to managing the world's monetary system. Camdessus conceded that "consensus amongst industrial and developing countries will be needed to design and carry out a reshaping of the international financial system". And one way to give developing countries a greater voice in IMF policymaking would be to grant more decision-making power to the IMF's Interim Committee.

The Interim Committee, which includes finance ministers and monetary officials from a wide range of countries, currently serves as an advisory body to the IMF's decision-making executive board, the membership of which is more restricted. Camdessus, in October

1998, said that "Reform proposals may receive added momentum at the annual, high-level meetings of finance ministers to be held by the IMF and World Bank over the next two weeks in Washington, DC."

Though Camdessus repeated the IMF's staunch support for allowing capital to flow across national borders unimpeded by government controls, he suggested possible private-sector approaches to managing the flows. Government controls over capital flows have gained new favour in the wake of the financial turmoil that has spread from Asia to Russia and Latin America since July 1997. But, Camdessus says, such controls are "not desirable, nor even feasible ... [nor] in any country's best interest."

"Resolving crises if they do occur requires earlier and deeper private-sector engagement ... especially when there is a large debt overhang.

"Many ideas are under consideration, including allowing majority voting in bond contracts to facilitate bond-holder agreement for rescheduling [of debt]."

And now that the IMF is working with member governments and other international institutions to strengthen the architecture of the global financial system, we are beginning to see glimmers of light at the end of the tunnel. "The world cannot wait ... for a lull before starting a better job at crisis prevention," Camdessus reiterated.

Conclusion

The Asian crisis has spawned a loss of faith in international institutions and a desperate search for alternatives to orthodox prescriptions. Dr Mahathir's imposition of so-called "high-stakes" experiment with capital controls on September 1, 1998 was simply a consequence of his frustration by the failure of textbook liberalisation measures to avert a recession.

The crisis has manifested weaknesses in the world's financial system. The system is now malfunctioning, with its built-in mechanisms—like the IMF—looking frail and fatigued. Dr Mahathir's views have struck a chord throughout the region and beyond. It would be a mistake to dismiss Dr Mahathir's stand that the IMF must rethink its bailout tactics and its usual requirement for tight money and fiscal restraint, when typically, borrowers need credit and economies need fiscal pump-priming.

According to Fidel Ramos, the former president of the Philippines, "Whether one agrees or disagrees with the specific measures that Malaysia has taken to defend itself against the inherent instability of the global financial market, one must sympathise with Kuala Lumpur's effort to defend itself from what it sees as a kind of *laissez-faire* capitalism which is going out of control."

And now that there is widespread consensus for reform, a new international financial architecture should be pursued with urgency. We need tougher policy measures and action immediately, otherwise, a worldwide slump will consume us. Already almost half the world is affected by the Asian contagion and economic prospects are expected to get worse before they get better.

Malaysia is not prepared to wait indefinitely for global action which may come a little too late. Hence, its controversial capital and currency controls. Bold new measures are needed to restore stability in the world financial markets: incremental and piecemeal efforts are clearly inadequate. Unless this fact is recognised by the world community, there will never be a permanent solution to the meltdown. What we desperately need now is a concerted plan of action for lifting the global economic and financial malaise that will bring about enhanced growth, contain financial contagion and alleviate social distress and political turmoil triggered by the crisis. But, according to the *Asiaweek* of October 16, 1998, "... a bigger and more worrying reason for G7 inaction is one embarrassing but undeniable reality: the Crisis has left everyone clueless. Whatever success and prescience they may claim, the world's economic thinkers and policymakers are running out of solutions."

Malaysia must act fast and resolutely. Positive results are already clear for all to see and enjoy.

Chapter 7

THE CHANGING
GLOBAL & DOMESTIC
LANDSCAPE

THE international economic and financial landscape is rapidly changing. We are indeed living in chaotic yet exciting times. *But how will these dynamic and unprecedented global developments impact on us here in Malaysia?*

Perhaps the most significant global development is that the mighty US economy is now clearly affected by the Asian economic turmoil. The US Federal Reserve chairman, Alan Greenspan, was spot-on when he stated in early September 1998 that "the United States is unlikely to remain an oasis of prosperity in the face of the Asian currency crisis", the first time a senior official of the US establishment had publicly admitted that even the United States (which most American officials and academics thought would be immuned from the Asian currency contagion) could be adversely affected by the Asian crisis.

If only more precautions were taken earlier, things would not be as bad as now. If only the US authorities had been humble and more down to earth, they would have seen the writing on the wall and done more to resolve the Asian financial crisis when it first emerged.

After nearly three years, the US Federal Reserve cut its benchmark Federal funds interest rates thrice in less than two months: by 0.25 per cent to 5.25 per cent on September 29, 1998, another 0.25 per cent to 5.00 per cent on October 15, and another 0.25 per cent to 4.75 per cent on November 17!

Even the IMF has reversed their policies. The IMF had initially insisted on tight monetary policy and had caused its Asian clients like South Korea, Thailand and Indonesia, to go into deeper recession and social misery. The IMF should be charged for violating human rights to a better life, and their senior officials should resign.

Why has the United States reduced its interest rates, the IMF reversed its stand and is now pushing for lower interest rates worldwide! Because the United States must have dictated so, since with lower US interest rates, capital funds will now move away from the United States—unless interest rates around the world go down as well! Hence, the whole world was asked to lower interest rates.

The US economy will be more affected by the Asian economic crisis. Its competitive position is being eroded by cheaper Asian goods. Consequently, the US balance of payments deficit will worsen and its economy will slow down and unemployment will rise. Then the US authorities will do more to solve the world's financial problems—but apparently not until then!

Global Financial Reform

It is remarkable how there is now a changing tide in international opinion on the critical issue of reforming the world's financial architecture.

Just about a year ago, at the 1997 Annual Meeting of the World Bank and the International Monetary Fund, Prime Minister, Dato' Seri Dr Mahathir Mohamad's call for global financial reform was a cry in the wilderness. It was rejected as far-fetched.

Now President Clinton himself has called for financial reform to be considered by the G7 countries. The Commonwealth Finance Ministers have already supported ideas to regulate disruptive short-term capital flows; US$1 trillion go round the world every day. Its like a tornado that can destroy everything in its path. And yet the United States and some rich countries from which these destructive hurricanes originate, did not care until the United States faced the crisis of the Long-Term Capital Management hedge fund, which the US financial system promptly bailed out.

But this new trend towards global financial reform will not be effective unless three issues are looked into:

First, there must be a radical review and possibly a new Bretton Woods system. Mere tinkering of the present discredited financial infrastructure will not do at all. It will be cosmetic and callous.

Second, the leadership in the IMF must change. The Managing Director Michel Camdessus has strenuously defended the IMF action in East Asia and Russia as appropriate—even after the record shows the IMF's dismal record. The US Congress that characteristically has not paid up its dues of US$18 billion, could perhaps settle its international obligations and at the same time insist that Camdessus be replaced by another major IMF shareholder from Europe or even Japan.

Third, international civil servants in the IMF and the World Bank should also be disciplined for making political statements publicly on individual countries.

Fancy the World Bank's Chief Economist, Joseph E. Stiglitz, recently suggesting publicly that Malaysia could face international sanctions, for introducing currency controls as in the case of South Africa during the apartheid era! What has the World Bank come to, if it can tolerate irresponsible statements like this from an international civil servant. Only the President of the World Bank could, if at all, make these kind of disparaging statements, if the integrity and the international self-respect of these multinational institutions are to be maintained and raised.

The United States Must Lead

It is gratifying that finally the United States President Bill Clinton himself has come out to say, "This country must lead. We've got to be aggressive. We've got to stay on the balls of our feet!"

However, it is sad that President Clinton has sat on balls as he dilly dallied in his efforts to lead because of his improper dalliance with Monica Lewinsky!

So much time has been wasted and so many lives lost in the countries ravaged by the Asian economic crisis and contagion—all because the United States and some rich industrial countries did not have the bells to ring out a new Bretton Woods system or to regulate rogue currency manipulators mainly from their rich countries.

However, the G7 met secretly to decide what they can do to save themselves from the Asian contagion and a possible worldwide recession. But nothing worthwhile came out of the G7 meeting except to defend themselves and their vested, narrow self-interests.

The IMF-World Bank annual meeting has now come out with a proposal to study the measures based on the US Secretary of Treasury Robert Rubin's ideas under the US-proposed international financial architecture.

There is clear testimony that the United States can lead if it wants to and that the Western world follows the US dictates, while the developing world just has to accept what is passed down. But we have little choice and practically no alternative. Therefore, we have to do what is best for us and to heck with calls from the rich and powerful oligarchists that we must comply with their standards which are meant to perpetuate their power and their domination over the poor ex-colonial developing countries. It is encouraging that then well-known American thinker, Lyndon LaRouche, has blamed the oligarchists in the United States, Canada and the United Kingdom for their conspiracy to suppress and dominate the world, especially the emerging economies of the South.

The mid-October 1998 meeting of US ambassadors and senior officials in Singapore gave the impression that the United States really does not care. The meeting was led by Stanley Roth, one of the US State Department's highest officials for East Asian Affairs, and Admiral Joseph Prueher, Commander-in-Chief of the US forces in the Pacific. Thus it was a pretty powerful gathering of top US officials, who interestingly "exchanged views on economic, political and security developments in the region". This indicates that the United States uses economic issues for its political and security interests as well. It is all part of a grand strategy to dominate Asia. Why would the US State Department meet with their economic as well as defence top brass to discuss this geo-political agenda.

The US Ambassador to Singapore, Steven Green, told the press that the desire of US business and investors to put money back into Southeast Asia was "tremendous"—but that they would remain cautious until the region's financial systems are "properly reformed". Unfortunately, his statement reeks of hypocrisy and double standards or what the Native Americans would describe as "white man speaks with fork tongue"!

What about the fundamental need for the United States itself to initiate major financial reforms in the United States and in the financial reforms and in the international financial system? If the United States had sound financial systems, the great debacle of the Long-Term Capital Management hedge fund would not have occurred and threatened to undermine the very foundations of the US financial system. That is why LTCM had to be bailed out to prevent what Greenspan believed would cause serious systemic problems in the US financial structure.

What about the "blemishes" in the US financial system? Why does US Ambassador Steven Green only talk about blemishes in the Southeast Asian region? Does he not realise that the Asian currency crisis exploded with the currency attacks mainly from US currency and hedge-fund manipulators? Or is it more convenient and strategic to dwell on finan-

cial blemishes in Asia to distract attention from the US strategy to dominate Asia through currency attacks and other means.

This theory is borne out well by the claim of Shintaro Ishihara, the colorful and outspoken Japanese politician and author of *The Japan That Can Say No*, in the *Asiaweek* of October 16, 1998: "Looking back on the panic triggered by the currency crisis in Thailand and the inroads made by the International Monetary Fund (IMF), we can see the subtle strategy America is employing to dominate the world." The United States should lead as it is the most powerful country today, but it should lead for the good of the world and not for its own self-interests alone.

US Human Rights

Amnesty International Secretary-General Pierre Savé has called the United States "hypocritical and deteriorating human-rights situation on his visit to Mexico in October 1998.

The United States has been nagging every country on human rights, including China, when President Clinton visited it earlier this year.

But the 1998 Amnesty International Report has stated that in the United States itself there is widespread police brutality, inhuman treatment, abuse of asylum seekers and minority races and the infringement of various international laws.

Pierre Savé had gone to Mexico to persuade that country to put pressure on the United States—its neighbour and fellow member of NAFTA, to improve its far from luminous human-rights record. But Mexico, like most other countries, especially the developing countries, are afraid to criticise the Americans! *Why?* Because the Americans will use their vast powers as the only superpower in the world, to undermine any country that dares to criticise the United States.

Malaysia has been criticizing the United States for its record of hypocrisy and double standards for a long time—and that is why the

United States has used its influence through the Western print and broadcast media to discredit Malaysia at every opportunity.

The Third World countries are like all other countries, not perfect. We have our own weaknesses in the field of human rights that must be addressed. But what is resentful and even detestable is the "holier-than-thou" attitude of the United States and many Western countries, when their own human-rights track record is so dismal— despite their far greater state of socio-economic development and evolution in national governance.

G7 Fails

Despite the high expectations that the exclusive Group of Seven (G7) of the world's richest countries, will make policy decisions to help solve the current Asian financial crisis—nothing really happened. The G7 meeting in Washington in October 1998 was disappointing and a huge failure.

The G7 recognised that the Asian economic crisis could cause risks to their own economic growth but did not address the major cause of the Asian crisis which is the weak international financial architecture. They did not even mention the need to introduce some regulation of the rogue currency speculators and manipulators.

Even the leading currency speculator George Soros mentioned that the G7 Statement sounded a little bit empty", before attending the 1998 IMF Annual Meeting in Washington in October 1998.

It is thus clear that the rich countries really do not want to move until they are bitten even more severely by the Asian contagion bug.

The LTCM fiasco has not yet taught the United States a lesson. While the United States condemned Asian countries for their weak financial institutions, crony capitalism, corruption and financial mismanagement, the US authorities practised wholesale cronyism to bail out the LTCM with a huge capital injection of US$3.5 billion. Bankers allowed LTCM to run a peak exposure of US$200 billion against an equity capital of only US$4.8 billion. *This must be the classic example of colossal crony capitalism at work.*

It is also very ironical that Federal Reserve's Chairman Alan Greenspan approved the bail out of LTCM, thus giving the US government's blessings. We can clearly see double standards at work here.

Perhaps people who live in glass houses should not throw stones. The United States has shown itself to be quite incapable of practising the high moral standards it preaches—from its highest officials (President Clinton) right down the line!

The Changing Domestic Scene: Balance of Trade

On the domestic front, it is encouraging that Malaysia's trade balance for the first 8 months of this year rose to RM32.4 billion. The Department of Statistics, however, does not state how much of this increase is due to genuine increase in the volume of our exports and how much of the increase is due to the depreciation of the ringgit.

The credibility of the Department of Statistics could be raised further if the department could in future give a more professional presentation of its balance of payments accounts.

The Department of Statistics' standing could also be enhanced if it gave a commentary on the underlying implications of the figures that are published.

The imports grew by only 12.5 per cent as compared to the increase in exports by a whopping 38.6 per cent! Undoubtedly a significant position of this increase can reasonably be attributed to the depreciation of the ringgit, which also caused a severe decline in imports due to the higher import prices.

What is striking, however, is that intermediate goods rose by RM19.4 billion or 21.8 per cent over the first 8 months of 1998. Here again it is not clear as to how much of this increase is due to mere price increases. But it is telling that if adjustments are made to the exchange rate of the ringgit, it would appear that the imports of intermediate goods have slowed down considerably.

Thus, Malaysia's industrial capacity to produce goods for export could have reduced considerably. The adverse effects will show up in the future. It also indicates that the government's reflation or expansionary policies have not really taken off as expected. If the additional funds allocated for development expenditures had been utilised, the import bill for intermediate goods like machinery and equipment would have been higher.

Overall, although the trade balance has improved, it must be realised that this positive development may not be sustained in the longer term—if the volume of exports have not really grown and if the imports of intermediate goods have slowed down.

In the meantime, however, it is better to have a trade surplus rather than a trade deficit. But we'll have to work much harder to ensure that those trade surpluses grow stronger and are sustained. Otherwise, confidence will be slow to rise and the earlier weakness in the balance of payments, which like blood attracted the currency sharks, could still remain.

New Monetary Policies

Bank Negara Malaysia has announced the large recapitalisation of 14 banking institutions, and the encouraging decline of non-performing loans (NPLs) from 15.8 per cent to 9.7 per cent. It has also reduced the capital adequacy and solvency margin requirements for insurance companies. These announcements will strengthen confidence and encourage more openness and transparency.

It is significant that Bank Negara Malaysia has also stated that Danamodal would be recapitalising fourteen banking institutions as part of its first phase. Most Malaysians would not have realised that so many banks are in so much trouble. This begs the question as to how so many banks took "moral hazard" for granted and got into trouble. *What were these top bankers doing to allow their banks to slide? What is the assurance that these and other troubled banks will reform and become more accountable for more efficiency and better performance? Will good money be chasing bad money?* The people have the right to know and to be assured by Bank Negara Malaysia that these banks and bankers will not fail us all again. Some banks have already failed us again and again. We have to stop this lack of responsibility.

Bank Negara Malaysia will have to insist on higher standards and ensure that the best bankers are selected to run these banks. If we cannot get sound bankers at home, let us get them from abroad. Its better to hire professional foreigners than to have our banks fail again through poor local managers. Then our banks will be taken over by foreign banks, under the pressure of the WTO. We should avoid this threat.

The people would appreciate if Bank Negara Malaysia could list out these weak banks and provide periodic indicators of the performance of our banks. This way our banks will be forced to become more competitive. This will strengthen our financial system to resist future external currency attacks! If our financial institutions were stronger I am sure that our economy would have been in a better position to weather the battering storms of the currency speculators and manipulators.

Now that we are "insulated" from these currency attacks, I hope that our financial system and institutions are thoroughly reformed. Otherwise, we will not have gained from the respite or breathing space provided by the capital and currency controls and our current "insulation" from currency attacks. That would be disastrous! Let us not repeat the mistakes of the past. We must come down hard on weak banks and bankers.

Renong Debt Restructuring

The RM10.5 billion rescue plan for Renong has been cleverly packaged by Credit Suisse First Boston. There is much relief that this rescue plan has been agreed in principle by the government. Now the great doubts and fears about the future of Renong and UEM and their adverse financial impact on the whole banking system could perhaps be removed.

These strategic *Bumiputera* companies will be saved and the banking system will be strengthened, with the issue of government-guaranteed bonds to be issued by the new unit of the Ministry of Finance called the Infrastructure Development Corporation.

As to whether this exercise is a "borrowing to bail out" strategic companies is not the issue. After all, this financial rescue strategy is not new. The recent Long-Term Capital Management Fund bailout in the United States was much larger. LTCM had an exposure of US$200 billion against an equity capital of only US$4.8 billion! So the rescue of Renong is relatively insignificant. But what is significant is the impact of the lessons learnt from this rescue on our economic management.

Lessons Learnt

First, the rescued Renong must now be much more stringent and prudent. We have to learn the fundamental lesson of cutting our coat according to our cloth. Do not be over-ambitious and overborrow, especially when we are dealing with publicly raised funds.

Second, we must ensure that some of the management in the rescued companies will not continue to serve the company. The people cannot afford to have business leaders who can get off scot-free for their major business failures. These companies must learn to restructure themselves and change their managers and management styles!

Third, we have to realise that borrowing RM10.5 billion through bonds, denies these funds to improve the welfare of the poor and less fortunate in our society. The National Development Policy (NDP) is concerned with corporate restructuring as well as poverty eradication. By spending so much on restructuring, we will be allocating less resources to poverty eradication and society's welfare. Many more schools, hospitals and agricultural projects and programmes could be provided for the poor and deserving, from the billions that will be raised from our savings to rescue weak companies.

After all, despite the creditable fact that we have one of the highest savings rate in the world at about 40 per cent of the GNP, there are nevertheless limitations. *How much can we borrow and save and divert away from the poverty sectors of the Malaysian economy?* We can only hope that this will be the last major rescue plan and that there will be no more huge corporate surprises.

Bank Negara Malaysia's New Image

While the IMF itself has become more transparent, Bank Negara Malaysia's stance is becoming more open. Its image is more communicative and more realistic, and may be the IMF should take its cue from Bank Negara Malaysia. The new Governor, Tan Sri Ali Abul Hassan Sulaiman's more frequent press briefings are helping the public and foreign investors understand and appreciate the new monetary moves. These new monetary measures are raising public and business confidence due to Bank Negara Malaysia's more pragmatic approach to monetary governance. This new policy stance belies the cynical and negative remarks of Western analysts like Bruce Gale of the Political & Economic Risk Consultancy (PERC) in Singapore over CNBC Asia recently that Bank Negara Malaysia's credibility is questioned due to its so-called "flip-flop policies". Surely changing policies to suit Malaysia's needs is a sign of dynamic management—even if it is not of the IMF kind. We should not rigidly stick to policies that benefit foreigners and not our national interests!

It is shocking how bitterly reactionary some of these so-called experts can become when their rigid Western-based orthodoxy is challenged by innovations such as exchange controls that surely undermine their narrow aim to merely profit from the liberal monetary systems that their clients can exploit. Their consultancy fees can of course be seriously eroded—but one would hope that these consultants would at least be more objective and professional! CNBC Asia have a duty to the public to be truthful and objective and not have a hidden agenda!

Conclusion

The currency attacks of mid-1997 and the resultant Asian financial crisis have been changing the global and domestic landscape. There will be more changes in the months ahead, hopefully for the better, as hard-headed free traders and currency speculators and manipulators are forced to change their thinking brought about by the realities of the damages they have caused to developing countries, global economic growth and financial stability.

The developing countries too have undergone much changes. There will now be greater realisation that we are operating in a global village and that any indiscipline or indiscretion in one country can have systemic and destructive effects soon other countries.

There must be a new world order, one that is mutually beneficial, with a new Bretton Woods agreement for a new global financial architecture.

The rich and powerful industrial countries of the North and the poorer economies of the South must work out a New Deal based on a rewarding smart partnership of "prospering thy neighbour", so that the 21st century will provide a better and more equitable world society for all.

Chapter 8

AN EXPANSIONARY BUDGET TO RESUSCITATE THE ECONOMY

LIKE the good doctor that he is, Dato' Seri Dr Mahathir Mohamad, the Prime Minister and the First Minister of Finance, prescribed proposals in the 1999 Budget to revitalise the ailing Malaysian economy. The Budget is seen by many as a continuation of an overall plan to get the economy back on track by restoring investor confidence and strengthening national resilience.

The good news is that we could be out of the recession by the end of 1999 with a positive growth of 1 per cent as compared to a negative 4.8 per cent growth estimated for 1998. However, we cannot take this projected recovery for granted. As Dr Mahathir has pointed out, our recovery will depend on the effectiveness of implementing the new Budget proposals and the National Economic Recovery Plan (NERP). Our success also depends on the regional and world economic outlook, which were not so good, but are now improving, with the reduction of interest rates in the United States and elsewhere.

Nevertheless, we have to put our shoulders to the wheel and soldier on together with determination and diligence, and to work even harder for more stable political conditions, especially in view of the trial of Dato' Seri Anwar Ibrahim.

The 1999 Budget was a difficult Budget to design amidst current recessionary pressures. The Prime Minister's Treasury team, led by the Second Finance Minister and Minister of Entrepreneur Development, Dato' Mustapa Mohamed, deserves full praise for a fine budget. It was pragmatic, comprehensive and reflationary.

Questions

Although the Budget speech was what we needed for recovery, it nevertheless begs some questions of public interest, as follows:

First, the Budget's overall deficit of RM16.6 billion is large and will be financed by borrowing. However, it would be useful if more details are provided as early as possible as to the specific sources of this borrowing. General assurances are useful but not sufficient to allay concerns over the significant deficit financing. The Employees Provident Fund (EPF) will be the main source of financing the Budget deficit, since the EPF collects about RM1.2 billion every month from its contributors.

How much of the borrowing will be sourced from the EPF, local bonds, the government's realisable assets or even foreign borrowing?

With Danamodal and Danaharta having to raise RM16 billion and RM15 billion respectively there can be difficulties in harnessing adequate funds to finance the large overall deficit. Then there is the additional requirement of RM5.5 billion for the 23 companies that have applied for debt relief from the Corporate Debt Restructuring Committee.

Second, debt servicing has already risen to about 14 per cent of the federal government's operating expenditure. This is the second highest expenditure item after the 21 per cent allocated for salaries.

We will have to be careful that debt servicing does not rise too steeply. We have little alternative but to borrow to revitalise the economy, but we will have to monitor the rising debt and be careful that we do not overborrow. Excessive borrowing as we very well know can cause a "debt trap" in the future which will be difficult to escape. Thus we will have to ensure that government investments are not only cost effective but income generating as well. Otherwise, we will not have the income flows to finance debt servicing.

In fact, during the recession of the mid-1980s, we tried to borrow ourselves out of the recession but found it perilous as the recession lasted longer than expected. We then had to cut back on spending and borrowing. Under the stewardship of Tun Daim Zainuddin, who took over the reins of finance from Tengku Razaleigh Hamzah, we consolidated the economy and then recovered when the world economy picked up in the late 1980s. We need to reflate but we need to do so carefully and cautiously. Otherwise, deficit financing can become inflationary and result in socio-economic problems. That would be most destabilising and should be avoided as far as possible.

Third, the capital and currency controls were timely at a time when the ringgit and the stockmarket were under serious foreign attacks. The ringgit was then fixed at RM3.80 to the US dollar in September 1998. But the US dollar has since weakened. The ringgit, therefore, could be stronger than the current rate of RM3.80.

It is therefore good to have the assurance in the Budget speech that the government "will be flexible and pragmatic" in regard to the value of the ringgit.

However, it is time to review the value of the ringgit, now that the balance of payments have improved considerably and foreign-exchange reserves have also risen impressively. We could also have the value of the ringgit vary within a narrow band of, say, 5 per cent. This will still give stability for trade and investment and allow for some flexibility.

The exchange controls could be renamed "exchange stabilisation measures" in order to counter the wrong impressions and distortions abroad about our foreign-exchange controls. They are unfortunately or deliberately deemed as "isolationary" and not "insulation" from the highly volatile international financial system and the hazardous operations of hedge funds.

Some refinements could also be made to focus on regulating the speculative hot money. The Budget could have introduced a kind of Tobin tax and other measures tried and tested elsewhere (as in Chile), to counter sudden large short-term and reversible capital flows, which are manipulative and disruptive.

Furthermore, the stockmarket could be more buoyant if the one-year curb on taking out equity investment, could now be modified to keep and attract genuine long-term foreign equity investment, as opposed to keeping and attracting speculative short-term capital. These proposed revisions will underline the Budgets' commitment that the exchange controls are not permanent.

Fourth, the Budget preference to finance the continuation of privatised infrastructural projects and to rescue some financial institutions, will certainly help reflate the economy. But the government would certainly need to ensure good value for the large amounts of public money spent on these projects. The genuine rescue of some projects can turn out to be bad bailouts if the companies are chosen for the wrong reasons.

Orderly Liberalisation

The Budget speech states clearly that Malaysia remains committed to the market mechanism and the process of orderly liberalisation. There is no doubt that this is good. However, liberalisation implies globalisation. But, unfortunately, this is what caused the crisis in Thailand in the first place and then spread to the rest of Asia. So it is vital that we go for orderly—not rapid—liberalisation. Liberalisation without the appropriate instutional infrastructure is unlikely to be sustainable in the long term. We should not rush into globalisation head-on and open ourselves to the destructive capability of currency manipulators, who are currently unregulated and left to their own devices, to cause havoc as they choose.

We should have learnt the bitter lessons of rapid liberalisation. We should only liberalise our financial structures in tandem with the strengthening of our financial institutions, which are still not strong enough. We should also insist on the need for a new international financial architecture that is transparent. Thus we have to prepare to resist undue pressure from the United States and other APEC countries that will want us to liberalise rapidly to suit their own agenda for globalisation or what I call the *"gobble-isation"* of our institutions and assets.

As former US Secretary of State Dr Henry A. Kissinger wisely stated in his recent article "Perils of Globalisation" in the *Washington Post*, "to acquire control of Asian companies assets cheaply and to reconstitute them on the American model [would be] courting long-term disaster". The United States could benefit from Kissinger's sound advice! Unfortunately, the US administration is more likely to be influenced by Secretary of Treasury Robert Rubin who was formerly from Wall Street himself!

Improve Implementation

The Budget speech rightly points out that besides external factors, Malaysia's economic prospects will be determined by the speed of implementation of the economic recovery measures that the government has introduced. But there is not much that is indicated as to how our implementation capacity is to be improved. Productivity in the public service has to improve—but it's a pity Cuepacs is against working just 15 minutes more each day in exchange for holidays on Saturdays once a month!

To raise productivity, can the civil service be made more selective and more rewards be given for productivity and efficiency? Can bureaucracy be further reduced by removing the many unnecessary rules and regulations?

What about introducing a system of approvals which are *ex-ante*, instead of being *ex-poste*. For instance, can private professionals like architects, engineers and others, be given the authority to approve building plans, without waiting for the long delay in getting government approvals. Government officials can inspect the plans and buildings *ex-poste*, i.e. after the buildings are completed. Then, if there are violations of government rules and regulations, the private professionals could be severely punished and asked to compensate for their professional negligence and even struck off from their professional register, if necessary. This way, business will move at a faster pace, the private professionals will do a better job, and the government will be blamed less for the delay in approvals. This proposal should be given serious consideration.

The 1999 Budget provides the right prescription for recovery. However, there need to be some revision and refinements to our foreign exchange and other regulations, as well as our implementation capacity, in order to ensure and expedite our economic recovery.

The budget will most likely raise public confidence and provide relief for banks and businesses, but whether it will resuscitate the economic remains to be seen. Though the measures will arrest the downward spiral of the economy, we can expect a mild revival in 1999 if the many good Budget proposals and the NERP are effectively implemented. Hopefully the budget will be a harbinger of better things to come and put the economy on an even keel again towards sustainable growth and development.

APEC Summit in Kuala Lumpur

Malaysia's business and professional community, therefore, were assured when the 6th APEC Summit in Kuala Lumpur on November 17-18, 1998 did not introduce time frames for globalisation and liberalisation in the Early Voluntary Sectoral Liberalisation (EVSL) scheme that will undermine Malaysia's prospects for orderly economic development and progress. Malaysia could well be a minority voice, since IMF-aided countries are not able to say much. But the

Japanese opposed the EVSL and so the United States had to give in reluctantly, as there was no consensus. This issue will now be referred to the WTO, where the Europeans will no doubt oppose the United States as well.

The Asia-Pacific Economic Cooperation (APEC) Summit in Kuala Lumpur on November 17-18, 1998, though not exactly a smashing success for Malaysia, had its moments. However, it may not have been so successful for the United States and some other allied countries, as they did not have their way.

It appears that the United states, and, *inter alia*, Australia, Canada, New Zealand and the small island economies of Hong Kong and Singapore were keen to adopt the Early Voluntary Sectoral Liberalisation (EVSL) package for nine economic sectors. But the Japanese opposed the EVSL package because of their reservations over the fishery and forestry sectors, which are highly sensitive to the Japanese political economy.

The United States and some other countries tried to pressure the Japanese, but fortunately, the chairperson of the APEC Ministerial Summit, Malaysian Minister of Trade and Industry, Dato' Seri Rafidah Aziz, took a professional and neutral stand. Thus the United States had to back down, despite its usual attempts to ram down its views on others.

Malaysia on its part will continue to liberalise and globalise, but like the Japanese, we will do so at our own pace, although we were prepared to adopt the EVSL package, if necessary.

Malaysia's major success, however, was achieved in highlighting the need for urgent restructuring of the international financial architecture, especially in regulating currency speculators. Thus an APEC task force will be set up to review the operations of hedge funds and other financial institutions and develop practical proposals for the endorsement and implementation of APEC leaders, as early as possible. Though the role of hedge funds and financial speculation were major considerations in the debate, whether the summit's proposal to review the activities of hedge funds and other financial instituions will be effectively followed up, is another question to consider.

Dr Mahathir Mohamad's concern over the irresponsibility of international credit rating agencies was taken into account with the APEC call "for a review of their practices to promote greater effectiveness and to contribute to sustainable capital flows." Three of the major international rating agencies rapidly responded, though negatively, to the APEC call for the review of their transparency!

This will be another test of the credibility and relevance of APEC. If the United States, as the leader of the grouping, cannot ensure that this APEC decision is implemented, then APEC itself will be undermined and its participation and leadership will be perceived as mere rhetoric.

It is therefore hoped that the US and other developed or industrial countries in APEC will practise what they preach, and that APEC will indeed prove its relevance to promote trade and investment and economic growth and welfare for all countries and peoples within the grouping, and not only the interests of the few rich and powerful countries within the Asia-Pacific region. Only time will tell!

Though an outline of the crisis response emerged, there were no concrete or detailed measures or plans to avoid any global recession and no agreement on early trade liberalisation either. Hence the relevance of APEC can still be questioned.

Conclusion

I believe that with the effective implementation of the 1999 Budget proposals as well as the National Economic Recovery Plan, the Malaysian economy will heal and recover at the end of 1999, and start the year 2000 on a stronger footing. The wounded Malaysian tiger will leap forward and growl again despite some efforts from powerful foreign forces to undermine its independence as well as those of other developing countries.

The gradual realisation in the West that the United States and other industrial countries should themselves become more transparent in the supervision and operation of vast hedge funds like the United States' LTCM will go a long way towards improving the international financial architecture.

When the developed countries come round to accepting a more enlightened and equitable international financial system, only then will the whole world benefit from greater peace, stability and prosperity for all countries to enjoy the best that this good earth of ours has to offer.

SUGGESTED READING

Bhagwati, Jagdish (1998), "The Capital Mobility Myth," *Foreign Affairs*, May-June 1998, 77(3).

Cheng, Allen T. (1998), "The Global Manipulators," *Asian Inc*, November 1998, 7(4).

Chin, P.Y. (1998), "How the Hedge Fund Mutation Occurred," *Asia Inc*, November 1998, 7(4).

Dobbs-Higginson, M.S. (1996), *Asia-Pacific: Its Role in the New World Disorder*, London: Mandarin.

Drucker, Peter F. (1995), *Managing in a Time of Great Change*, New York: Dutton, Truman Talley Books.

Elegant, Robert (1990), *Pacific Century: The Rise of the East*, London: Headline.

Fallows, James (1994), *Looking at the Sun: The Rise of the New Asian Economic and Political System*, New York: Pantheon Books.

Garnaut, Ross (1996), *Open Regionalism and Trade Liberalization: An Asia-Pacific Contribution to the World Trade System*, Singapore: Institute of Southeast Asian Studies.

Gill, Ranjit (1998), *Asia Under Siege: How the Asian Miracle Went Wrong*, Singapore: Epic Management Services.

Godement, Francois (1998), *The Downsizing of Asia*, London: Routledge.

Huntington, Samuel P. (1993), "The Clash of Civilisations?," *Foreign Affairs*, 72: 3, 1993.

Huntington, Samuel P. (1996), *The Clash of Civilisations and the Remaking of World Order*, New York: Simon & Schuster.

Kissinger, Henry A. (1998), "Globalism Stoking Flames of Financial Disaster," *New Straits Times*, October 26, 1998.

Khoo, Boo Teik (1995), *Paradoxes of Mahathirism: An Intellectual Biography of Mahathir Mohamad*, Kuala Lumpur: Oxford University Press.

Krugman, Paul (1994), "The Myth of Asia's Miracle," *Foreign Affairs*, November-December 1994, 73(6).

Krugman, Paul (1997), "What Ever Happened to the Asian Miracle?," *Fortune*, August 18, 1997.

Krugman, Paul (1994), *Peddling Prosperity: Economic Sense and Nonsense in the Age of Diminished Expectations*, New York: W.W. Norton & Co.

Lingle, Christopher (1998), *The Rise & Decline of the Asian Century: False Starts on the Path to the Global Millennium*, Hong Kong: Asia 2000.

Mahathir Mohamad & Shintaro Ishihara (1995), *The Voice of Asia: Two Leaders Discuss the Coming Century*, Tokyo: Kodansha International.

Mahathir Mohamad (1998), *The Challenges of Turmoil*, Malaysia: Pelanduk Publications.

McLeod, Ross & Ross Garnaut (eds.) (1998), *East Asia in Crisis: From Being a Miracle to Needing One?*, London: Routledge.

Mertens, Brian (1998), "Asia's Exports Miss the Boat," *Asian Business* 34(10), October 1998.

Montes, Manuel F. (1998), *The Currency Crisis in Southeast Asia*, Singapore: Institute of Southeast Asian Studies.

Navaratnam, Ramon V. (1997), *Managing the Malaysian Economy: Challenges & Prospects*, Malaysia: Pelanduk Publications.

Navaratnam, Ramon V. (1998), *Strengthening the Malaysian Economy: Policy Changes & Reforms*, Malaysia: Pelanduk Publications.

Radelet, Steven & Jeffrey D. Sachs (1997), "Asia's Re-emergence," *Foreign Affairs*, November-December 1997.

Reyes, Alejandro & Tim Healy (1998), "Shattered Summit: What Went Wrong in Kuala Lumpur, and Why," *Asiaweek*, November 27, 1998.

Sachs, Jeffrey D. (1997), "Asia's Miracle is Alive and Well," *Time*, September 29, 1997.

Sachs, Jeffrey D. (1998), "The IMF and the Asian Flu," *The American Prospect*, March-April 1998.

Schumpeter, Joseph A. (1951), *The Theory of Economic Development*, Cambridge: Harvard University Press.

INDEX

Tan Sri Ramon V. Navaratnam is a distinguished former civil servant and corporate personality. He was an Economist with the Malaysian Treasury for 27 years, where he rose to become its Deputy Secretary-General. During that time, he also served as Alternate Director on the Board of Directors of the World Bank in Washington, DC. He was also directly involved in the preparation of the Malaysian annual budgets and five-year economic development plans for many years. He then became the Secretary-General of the Ministry of Transport in 1986.

After retiring from the civil service in 1989, Navaratnam was appointed CEO of Bank Buruh for five years. He is now Corporate Adviser to the SungeiWay group of companies, Executive Director of Sunway College and a Director of the Asian Strategy and Leadership Institute. He continues to serve the Malaysian government as Vice-Chairman of the Malaysian Business Council and is also on the Board of Directors of Matrade.

Navaratnam is the author of *Managing the Malaysian Economy: Challenges & Prospects* (1997) and *Strengthening the Malaysian Economy: Policy Changes & Reforms* (1998).

What *Managing the Malaysian Economy:*
Challenges & Prospects is all about:

THIS book discusses the challenges and prospects that lie ahead as Malaysia marches towards the new millennium and beyond. The rapid economic growth Malaysia enjoyed since the mid-1980s is a fact that is hard to ignore. The economy has in fact averaged 8 per cent per annum for the last 8 years. Economists have expressed concern about inflation, but at 3-4 per cent per annum, it is still well under control.

This book encourages a critical and distinctively Malaysian approach to the problems the country face as it strives towards developed-nation status by the year 2020. Malaysia's plan now is to go for productivity-driven growth with sustainable external balance and price stability. And despite Malaysia's inherent problems of a labour force that is becoming increasingly scarce and costly, Malaysia will continue to be attractive to foreign investors in the years to come because of its political stability, good infrastructure and an English-speaking workforce. Malaysia's continued success will now depend on its ability to attract technologically advanced industries and continuing strong leadership.

ISBN 967-978-581-5

What the reviews say of
*Managing the Malaysian Economy:
Challenges & Prospects*

"... a thought-provoking book. ... Navaratnam looks at the challenges facing Malaysia squarely and to his credit has come forward with many practical solutions to some of the excesses and hangovers from the prolonged economic boom." *The Star*

"... a book worth reading ... this book ... stimulates public discussion of Malaysia's major economic issues and the associated challenges and prospects. It ... offers criticisms and suggestions that reflect the concerns of a moderate, independent, pragmatic and visionary Malaysian nationalist who wishes to see the continued growth and development of the country." *New Straits Times*

"... a must-read for the business visitor to the country who could use a clear, insightful summation of why Malaysia is likely to be the country that will prosper longest and best amidst Southeast Asia's ascendancy. ... might be good for investors, but it is even better for Malaysians." *Malaysian Business*

"... reviews the diversity of challenges and prospects facing the Malaysian economy as it approaches the second millennium. The binding metaphor of this collection of pieces is management of the economy of Malaysia as it traverses the watershed to become an industrialised nation." *Management*

"Though not everyone may agree with Navaratnam's stance on the environment, the average businessman would probably concur with the need to advocate productivity-driven growth. ... His book is retrospective, emphasising the strengths in Malaysia's economic planning since Merdeka." *Malaysian Industry*

What *Strengthening the Malaysian Economy:
Policy Changes & Reforms* is all about:

THIS book attempts to provide solutions to Malaysia's economic malaise as it strives to become an industrialised nation. The Malaysian economy, which had enjoyed spectacular growth for eight consecutive growth, was jolted from its euphoria in July 1997, when the vicious contagion effect arising from the *de facto* devaluation of the Thai baht send East Asian currencies and stockmarkets nosediving to lows the likes of which have never been seen before. Why was this breathtaking march to prosperity brought to a grinding halt by the financial crisis? What were the probable causes of the crisis and what lessons can be drawn from it?

Though Malaysia has turned the corner in grappling with the financial crisis, tough times still lie ahead. Reforms will take time to be implemented and results will not be forthcoming. A change in mindset is crucial: the crisis must be seen as an opportunity to work towards a more productivity-driven economy. A commitment to reforms and an understanding of how they are to be implemented are vital in expediting recovery and sustaining economic growth. Despite the uncertainty over how long the downturn will last, Malaysia's long-term prospects are still encouraging.

ISBN 967-978-642-0

What the review says of
*Strengthening the Malaysian Economy:
Policy Changes & Reforms*

"... a thought-provoking book. ... Navaratnam looks at the challenges facing Malaysia squarely and to his credit has come forward with many practical solutions to some of the excesses and hangovers from the prolonged economic boom." *The Star*

"These informative [*Managing the Malaysian Economy: Challenges & Prospects* and *Strengthening the Malaysian Economy: Policy Changes & Reforms*] books by Tan Sri Ramon Navaratnam provide a comprehensive assessment of the manifold problems facing the Malaysian economy, ranging from social and economic issues to unethical professional practices, money politics, corruption and nepotism. These books are essential reading for the man in the street, for policymakers and for economists alike who desire a good understanding of the state of play and of the future outlook for the Malaysian economy. Our current position at the recessionary phase of the business cycle makes Navaratnam's contribution both pertinent and topical. The essays are skilfully written and are well pitched to stimulate public policy discussion and debate.

"In these two books, Navaratnam espouses a common-sense approach to economic policy. His approach is one of steering, gently nudging and carefully explaining. At all times his arguments appear cogent and sensible."

From a review by Wong Koi Nyen, Lecturer in Economics, and Robin Pollard, Head, School of Business and Information Technology, Monash University Sunway Campus